T0004224

This is Philip Payne at his best. Ski[ll]... makes it clear that "biblical womanh[ood]... careful analysis provides unshakea[ble]... both in the Bible and in the full freedom of women to serve however God has called them.

> **BETH ALLISON BARR,** James Vardaman Professor of History at
> Baylor University and bestselling author of *The Making of Biblical*
> *Womanhood: How the Subjugation of Women Became Gospel Truth*

No scholar of the New Testament and church has spent more energy in examining and explicating the role of women in leadership and teaching and preaching than Phil Payne. His scholarship is well-known and impeccably fair-minded. This book judiciously and pastorally unravels the tight threads woven by complementarians and weaves them into a fresh, new tapestry that is both biblical and pastoral. It will be for me the go-to book for lay folks who need a response to the complementarians.

> **SCOT MCKNIGHT,** Chair of New Testament, Northern Seminary

A glorious blend of biblical history and theological analysis, Payne systematically dismantles the logical failures used to distort God's Word intended for human flourishing. This book will bring enormous healing to the body of Christ. If you need a book that quickly and clearly exposes the failed teachings of male-headship arguments, *The Bible vs. Biblical Womanhood* is it! Respected by Christians the world over, Phil Payne's research opens new doors of leadership for women.

> **MIMI HADDAD,** PhD, president of CBE International

Profound scholarship broken down to be made lively, clear, and understandable for any reader who wants to know what the Bible says about one of the most challenging issues facing the church today.

> **H. G. M. WILLIAMSON,** Emeritus Regius
> Professor of Hebrew, University of Oxford

A compelling and highly readable case for the full equality of women and men. This remarkable book presents the best in New Testament scholarship for non-specialists.

> **HAROLD NETLAND,** professor of philosophy of religion and
> intercultural studies, Trinity Evangelical Divinity School

Philip Payne has produced a most readable book on a most controversial topic which brings clarity with lucid writing, careful explanation, and good organization. It contains new research that has yet to appear in print. This work is a most helpful contribution for helping evangelical Christians find their way through this thicket of controversial teachings. For an up to date, readable, and enjoyable presentation of the egalitarian case, this is the book to read.

PETER H. DAVIDS, PhD, BSCD, and chaplain,
Our Lady of Guadalupe Priory

A readable, well researched, well-reasoned book, demonstrating God's consistent support of women throughout the Bible. Comprehensive, logical, and clear, this book is an indispensable treatment of women in the Bible. I enthusiastically recommend it to anyone eager to hear God's high regard for women or anyone who wrestles with the Bible's teaching on women.

DR. GRACE Y. MAY, associate professor of biblical studies and director of the Women's Institute, William Carey International University

If any reader wants to understand the egalitarian view of subjects such as head covering or a woman's submission to her husband, this is the book to read. This is an easy-to-read and must-have book for any serious reader on the equality of man and woman in Christ.

KEUM JU JEWEL HYUN, founder and president, Matthew 28 Ministries, Inc. and adjunct professor of theology of work, Bakke Graduate University, Dallas, Texas.

Philip Payne does the job of a careful exegete in explaining the difference between a biblical view of women in God's purposes and an artificial and alien view listing all the things that women purportedly cannot do by jaundiced modern interpreters. Payne has done the hard slog of a detailed reading of the text, and he's got the receipts for how his rivals have misspent their efforts in treating the Bible as a mirror of their own patriarchal subculture. Payne is arresting as he is persuasive!

DR. MICHAEL F. BIRD, PhD, University of Queensland, academic dean and lecturer in theology, Ridley College, Melbourne, Australia

THE
BIBLE
VS.
BIBLICAL
WOMANHOOD

HOW
GOD'S WORD
CONSISTENTLY
AFFIRMS GENDER
EQUALITY

THE
BIBLE
VS.
BIBLICAL
WOMANHOOD

**HOW
GOD'S WORD
CONSISTENTLY
AFFIRMS GENDER
EQUALITY**

PHILIP B. PAYNE

ZONDERVAN®

ZONDERVAN STUDY RESOURCES

The Bible vs. Biblical Womanhood
Copyright © 2023 by Philip B. Payne

Requests for information should be addressed to:
Zondervan, *3900 Sparks Dr. SE, Grand Rapids, Michigan 49546*

Zondervan titles may be purchased in bulk for educational, business, fundraising, or sales promotional use. For information, please email SpecialMarkets@Zondervan.com.

ISBN 9780310140337 (audio)

Library of Congress Cataloging-in-Publication Data

Names: Payne, Philip Barton, author.
Title: The bible vs. biblical womanhood: how God's word consistently affirms gender equality / Philip B. Payne.
Description: Grand Rapids: Zondervan, 2023. | Includes index.
Identifiers: LCCN 2022047790 (print) | LCCN 2022047791 (ebook) | ISBN 9780310140306 (paperback) | ISBN 9780310140313 (ebook)
Subjects: LCSH: Sex role—Religious aspects—Christianity. | Man-woman relationships—Religious aspects—Christianity. | Equality—Biblical teaching. | Women—Biblical teaching. | Women in Christianity. | BISAC: RELIGION / Biblical Studies / Exegesis & Hermeneutics | RELIGION / Christian Living / Love & Marriage
Classification: LCC BS680.W7 P39 2023 (print) | LCC BS680.W7 (ebook) | DDC 262.14082—dc23/eng/20221207
LC record available at https://lccn.loc.gov/2022047790
LC ebook record available at https://lccn.loc.gov/2022047791

Cover design: Bruce Gore | Gore Studio, Inc.
Cover art: © Pawel Czerwinski / Unsplash; Kaidash / Shutterstock
Interior design: Kait Lamphere

Printed in the United States of America

23 24 25 26 27 LBC 7 6 5 4 3

CONTENTS

ABBREVIATIONS

ACO   *Acta conciliorum oecumenicorum* (ed. E. Schwartz; Berlin, 1914–)

BDAG   Bauer, Danker, Arndt, and Gingrich, *A Greek-English Lexicon of the New Testament*

BDB   Brown, Driver, Briggs, *A Hebrew and English Lexicon of the Old Testament*

CEB   Common English Bible

CEV   Contemporary English Version

Chantraine   *Dictionnaire étymologique de la Langue Grecque: Histoire des Mots*

CSB   Christian Standard Bible

ESV   English Standard Version

ERV   English Revised Version

HALOT   *The Hebrew and Aramaic Lexicon of the Old Testament*, 5-volume standard dictionary

ICC   International Critical Commentary

IGC As. Min.   H. Grégoire, *Recueil des Inscriptions grecques chrétiennes d'Asie Mineure* (Paris, 1922)

JB   Jerusalem Bible

KJV   King James Version

LCL   Loeb Classical Library

LSJ   Liddell Scott Jones McKenzie, *A Greek-English Lexicon*, standard classical Greek dictionary

LXX   Alfred Rahlfs, *Septuaginta*, Greek translation of the Hebrew Scriptures

MSG   *THE MESSAGE*

Moulton and Milligan   *The Vocabulary of the Greek Testament Illustrated from the Papyri and Other Non-Literary Sources*

NA[28]   Nestle-Aland, *Novum Testamentum Graece* (28th edition), standard Greek New Testament

NAB   New American Bible

NASB   New American Standard Bible

NEB   New English Bible

NET   New English Translation Bible

NFPF[1]   *Nicene and Post-Nicene Fathers, Series 1*

NIDNTT   *New International Dictionary of New Testament Theology* (4 vols.), word studies

NRSV   New Revised Standard Version

NTS   *New Testament Studies*

OTP   *Old Testament Pseudepigrapha* (ed. J. H. Charlesworth; 2 vols.; New York, 1983)

PG   J. P. Migne, *Patrologia Graeca* (161 vols.), Greek church fathers

PGL   Lampe, G. W. H., *A Patristic Greek Lexicon*

Preisigke   *Wörterbuch der griechischen Papyrusurkunden*

REB   Revised English Bible

RSV   Revised Standard Version

RSVCE   Revised Standard Version Catholic Edition

Str-B   H. Strack and P. Billerbeck, *Kommentar zum Neuen Testament aus Talmud und Midrasch*

TDNT   *Theological Dictionary of the New Testament* (ed. G. Kittel; 10 vols.), Greek word studies

TEV   Today's English Version (= Good News Bible)

UBS[5]   *The Greek New Testament* (United Bible Societies) 5th edition

Woodhouse   *English-Greek Dictionary: A Vocabulary of the Attic Language*

MY ODYSSEY

I used to believe in "biblical manhood and womanhood"—that God ordained male headship in the home and in the church, that wives must submit to their husbands, but that husbands do *not* have to submit to their wives.

I no longer believe in "biblical manhood and womanhood" because it is not biblical.

Like many Christians, I took for granted that the Bible supports gender hierarchy in the church and the home. I grew up in a happy home where my father was the head of the house. Women never preached in our church. Men made church decisions.

I learned to read, love, and believe the Bible as the inerrant Word of God from my father, J. Barton Payne, who devoted his life to studying and teaching Scripture. Nevertheless, I had no assurance that I would have eternal life until at a Christian camp as a junior high student I realized that God, who cannot lie, promised eternal life to all who believe in Jesus Christ (John 3:16; Titus 1:2). I fell on my knees and asked forgiveness for not believing God's promise in Scripture. I was overjoyed with assurance of faith, an assurance that has never left me because it is based on God's written Word.

During my junior year as a pre-med student, I had the joy

of seeing a blind boy named Joel transformed by faith in Jesus Christ beyond anything medicine could do. So, with honors in literature and a growing love of the Bible, instead of going to medical school, I served for fourteen months as a "helping hand" missionary in Japan with The Evangelical Alliance Mission. My pastor in Nagoya told me that the greatest need of the evangelical church in Japan was someone with a PhD in New Testament, preferably from Cambridge University. So, after finishing my MA in New Testament and MDiv at Trinity Evangelical Divinity School, I entered the New Testament PhD program at Cambridge.

I chose to research Jesus's interpretation of the Parable of the Sower because in seminary I found no answer to arguments that the interpretation contradicts the parable and so could not have been taught by Jesus. As I directly confronted this challenge to my faith, I discovered that each reason given against its authenticity, when examined in Jesus's historical and linguistic context, actually supports that Jesus taught this parable interpretation.[1]

About a month after arriving in Cambridge, a lecturer stated, "No passage in the New Testament, understood in its original context, limits the ministry of women." I almost stood up and shouted, "That's not true."

I thought 1 Tim. 2:12's prohibition of women teaching men was the perfect refutation. So that evening I read 1 Timothy in Greek and continued to do so repeatedly for over a month. I was struck by the letter's pervasive concern with false teaching. Since women are the only people 1 Timothy identifies as deceived by the false teaching, this explains why Paul prohibited women in Ephesus from seizing authority to teach a man. Realizing that 1 Tim. 2:12 does not disprove the lecturer's statement, I began to examine every other passage about women in the Bible. Forty-nine years of research later, I still have not found any original

My Odyssey • xiii

passage of the Bible that prohibits women from engaging in any church ministry.

The Bible's teaching matters on this issue because the Bible is the Word of God, authoritative for all Christians.[2] And if God teaches it, that settles it. The Bible, not contemporary culture, should guide what we believe and how we live.

While I still believe that the Bible is inerrant, I no longer believe in "biblical manhood and womanhood." My view did not change because I rejected the authority of Scripture. My view changed because I examined the very Bible passages that I thought established gender hierarchy. It is precisely those passages, including 1 Cor. 11:2–16, 1 Cor. 14:34–35, Ephesians 5, 1 Timothy 2–3, Titus 1–2, and 1 Peter 3 that caused me to reject the exclusion of women from leadership in the church and the home.

Of course, given its cultural setting, the Bible has many examples of men in leadership, and far fewer of women in leadership. It describes the creation of the first human as male and Israel's official priests as male. Most of the identified authors of Scripture are male (see seven exceptions below, p. 25). Jesus is male and chose twelve male apostles. God is addressed as Father. Some consider this sufficient evidence that God desires a hierarchy of males in authority over women.

However, when we look more closely, we find that the Bible emphasizes:

- the Holy Spirit gifts all believers for ministry
- the oneness of the body of Christ (the church) and the priesthood of all believers
- the humility, service, and mutual submission required of all believers

These principles are where the biblical emphasis lies, and Scripture never teaches that men and women have separate "roles." We should not infer from the Bible's descriptions of patriarchal societies that it endorses patriarchy any more than its descriptions of polygamy endorse polygamy. The Greek texts of Ephesians 5 and 1 Peter 3 that supposedly teach male headship and female subordination actually teach mutual voluntary yielding in love. Passages that stress the equality of men and women, including Romans 16, 1 Corinthians 7, 1 Cor. 11:11–12, and Gal. 3:28, are not exceptions to the rule of male headship. They express the Bible's consistent, harmonious message of gender equality. No word meaning *headship* ever occurs in the Greek or Hebrew texts of Scripture.

This book explains how the text of Scripture itself affirms gender equality. Its emphasis is Christ-like service. Scripture, and Paul in particular, fights tenaciously for groups who are being excluded from full fellowship or denied equal rights. I approach this topic with a dual perspective: as a biblical scholar who has been a supervisor of New Testament studies in colleges of the University of Cambridge and who has taught New Testament at Trinity Evangelical Divinity School, Gordon-Conwell Theological Seminary, Bethel Seminary, and Fuller Theological Seminary; and as a missionary with the Evangelical Free Church in Japan. This book simplifies my 511-page book on this topic, *Man and Woman, One in Christ*.[3] It puts cookies on the lower shelf for everyone to enjoy. Although not examining passages in as much detail, this book includes my more recent discoveries and also examines Titus 2 and 1 Peter 3. It also tells many personal stories that highlight the significance of the Bible's teachings about man and woman.

NOTES

1. Philip B. Payne, "The Order of Sowing and Ploughing in the Parable of the Sower," NTS 25 (1977–78): 123–29; "The Seeming Inconsistency of the Interpretation of the Parable of the Sower," NTS 26 (1979–80): 564–68; "The Authenticity of the Parable of the Sower and its Interpretation," in *Gospel Perspectives: Studies of History and Tradition in the Four Gospels*, ed. R. T. France and David Wenham (Sheffield: JSOT, 1980), 163–207; "The Authenticity of the Parables of Jesus," *Gospel Perspectives II* (1981): 329–44.

2. Church fathers affirm the total trustworthiness of Scripture, including Clement of Rome (AD 90): "You have studied the Holy Scriptures, which are true, and given by the Holy Spirit. You know that nothing unjust or counterfeit is written in them" (1 Clement 45:2–3). Leo XIII's encyclical, *Providentissimus Deus*, affirms: "It is so impossible for divine inspiration to contain any error that, by its very nature, it not only excludes even the slightest error but must of necessity exclude it, just as God, the Supreme Truth, must also necessarily be absolutely incapable of promoting error." It concludes: "Consequently, any who were to admit that there might be error in the authentic pages of the sacred books ... make[s] God himself the author of error." *Dei Verbum*, the Second Vatican Council's Constitution on Divine Revelation, affirms regarding the Bible: "Inspired by God and committed once and for all to writing, they import the Word of God himself without change [no. 21] ... called by theologians 'inerrancy.'"

3. Described at www.pbpayne.com, where it is available at 40% off.

WHY DOES IT MATTER?

D oes it really matter whether or not "biblical womanhood" is biblical? If this is a secondary matter, should we cause division in the church by discussing this controversial topic? Many have doubts about gender hierarchy but don't talk about it to avoid causing division or being rejected.

Many Christians had concerns about slavery, but failed to speak up lest they cause division in the church. We now know that was a terrible mistake, and virtually all Christians embrace racial reconciliation and decry apartheid, slavery, and racial injustice. Nevertheless, people who limit women's ministry use many of the same Bible passages and interpret them in the same way that people did to support slavery. This should be a clear warning signal against that kind of interpretation.

I sympathize with those who fear causing division, for I waited—perhaps too long—to publish my research that demonstrates the Bible's support for gender equality, not gender hierarchy. After many years of research, I prayed that the Lord would give me specific guidance concerning whether or not I should publish my findings. Within twenty-four hours of that prayer, three events occurred that convinced me that God was guiding me to share that research. First, the president of my denomination,

A. T. Olson of the Evangelical Free Church of America, encouraged me to publish my findings. Second, the chairman of our Ministerial Association asked me to write a position paper on it. Third, someone gave me a *Trinity Journal* article arguing that women's "susceptibility to deception bars them from engaging in public teaching. . . . There are some activities for which women are by nature not suited."[1] I could hardly have asked for more clear guidance from God, so I began to publish my work. Scholars' endorsements of my discoveries and the spiritual freedom expressed by many readers have abundantly confirmed that this was, indeed, guidance from the Lord.

More important than how God guided me, this issue matters enough to study thoroughly because it affects the freedom of Christians to proclaim the gospel and advance God's kingdom. Prohibiting women from exercising their leadership and teaching gifts limits the proclamation of the gospel and the advancement of God's kingdom. It is not just a waste of resources. Many people hate the gospel because they associate it with the subjugation of women. God demands justice and prohibits favoritism and the subjugation of others. Gender hierarchy inherently entails favoritism and historically has been linked with the subjugation of women.[2] Furthermore, God commands us to seek the truth, individually and corporately, even if it takes diligent analysis to find it.

This book is primarily for those who care deeply about what the Bible teaches. It is especially for those struggling to reconcile the Bible's seemingly contradictory teachings about men and women. It is also for those who believe in gender hierarchy but who desire most of all to obey God's Word. Not everyone who supports gender equality (or gender hierarchy) also believes in biblical inerrancy, but whether or not every argument persuades you, I pray this book will enrich you.

NOTES

1. Douglas J. Moo, "1 Timothy 2:11–15: Meaning and Significance," *Trinity Journal* 1 (1980): 62–83, at 70. I responded with Philip B. Payne, "Libertarian Women in Ephesus: A Response to Douglas J. Moo's Article, '1 Timothy 2:11–15: Meaning and Significance,'" *Trinity Journal* 2 (1981): 169–197. Douglas J. Moo, "The Interpretation of 1 Timothy 2:11–15: A Rejoinder," *Trinity Journal* 2 (1981): 198–222, at 204 acknowledges, "The difficulties with viewing v 14 as a statement about the nature of women are real." The editor of *Trinity Journal*, Don Carson, refused to publish my surrejoinder, but it was published by the Committee on Ministerial Standing of the Evangelical Free Church of America as a supplement to *What Does the Scripture Teach about the Ordination of Women? Differing Views by Three New Testament Scholars: Dr. Walter L. Liefeld, Dr. Douglas Moo, Dr. Philip B. Payne*.

2. Kylie Maddox Pidgeon, "Complementarianism and Domestic Abuse: A Social-Science Perspective on Whether 'Equal but Different' is Really Equal at All," in *Discovering Biblical Equality: Biblical, Theological, Cultural, and Practical Perspectives*, 3rd ed., ed. Ronald W. Pierce and Cynthia Long Westfall (Downers Grove, IL: InterVarsity, 2021), 572–96.

MY DEFINITIONS OF INERRANCY, HIERARCHY, COMPLEMENTARY, AND BIBLICAL WOMANHOOD

Before discussing Bible passages in depth, it is helpful to explain how I use some key terms.

INERRANCY

Biblical inerrancy is misunderstood by many supporters and detractors alike. It does not advocate interpreting every Bible passage literally, regardless of its literary style or purpose.

The Chicago Statement on Biblical Inerrancy defines "inerrancy" as describing the original texts of Scripture as inspired by God, properly understood in light of their literary and cultural context. Article X affirms "that copies and translations of Scripture are the Word of God to the extent that they faithfully represent the original."[1] As Christian scholars since the time of Origen (circa AD 185–253) have understood, inerrancy acknowledges manuscript errors and later additions. Both my father and·I signed the original Chicago Statement on Biblical Inerrancy.

Our English-language Bibles are translations of edited texts of the Hebrew and Greek Scriptures based on thousands of old manuscripts. But none of the Greek and Hebrew manuscripts that translators use is *the* original manuscript of Galatians or Hosea, for example. Over thousands of years, we have lost the original manuscripts just as we have lost the original human authors. However, their message still survives. In spite of the diversity of the manuscripts, there is extensive continuity.

The scientific principles of textual criticism permit the reconstruction of the original text of the New Testament with remarkable reliability. This book applies those principles to the texts about women and demonstrates that our English Bibles often fail to convey their original meaning.

HIERARCHY

By "gender hierarchy" I mean a power relationship between women and men in which one gender is granted authority while the other is barred from serving in leadership roles. This stands in contrast to "gender equality," which means that women and men are equally welcome, based on their gifts and calling, to serve as leaders in the church and exercise shared authority in marriage. In short, "hierarchy" means uneven distribution of power, while "equality" means equal access to power.

Now, some proponents of gender hierarchy *claim* that they believe men and women are equal: they are both made in the image of God, have equal worth in God's sight, and so on. But when it comes to the everyday practice of leadership and use of power, they do not treat women as equal to men. When certain leadership roles are *only and always* limited to men, that is by definition gender hierarchy—in fact, it is a particular kind of gender hierarchy: patriarchy (rule by men).

Of course, in practice, churches and marriages that embrace gender equality will sometimes entrust leadership to a man and sometimes to a woman, depending on how God has gifted and called them. Men may lead, even most of the time, in such a church or marriage. Contrary to gender hierarchy, however, women in these churches and marriages *can* and are *welcome* to exercise any kind of authority and leadership according to their God-given gifts and calling.

COMPLEMENTARY

Many who defend gender hierarchy call themselves "complementarians" because they emphasize how men and women are different, made by God to complement one another.

I believe, as do all evangelicals I know who support gender equality, that God created women to complement men. Therefore this book puts "complementarians" in quotes. Nevertheless, some defenders of gender hierarchy give the false impression that egalitarians deny differences between women and men.[2]

Many defenders of gender hierarchy also give the false impression that only their view is true to the Bible. In fact, as we will see, the Bible is full of examples of God's Spirit guiding and equipping women to do things that their cultures reserved for men.

By restricting teaching and leadership roles in the church to men, gender hierarchists limit women's exercise of their

God-given gifts. By commanding women not to teach or lead men, some have urged women to disobey God's calling. By denying that Scripture calls women to exercise their teaching and leadership gifts in local churches, "complementarians" effectively deny Scripture's authority. When I read some of the abusive things gender "complementarians" have written about the egalitarian view and about women such as Beth Moore, whose ministry has blessed so many, I wonder if they have ever considered that they might be resisting the Holy Spirit (Acts 7:51; 13:45; 18:6 cf. Mark 3:29; Luke 12:10).

> Wayne Grudem, founder of The Council on Biblical Manhood and Womanhood, asserts "The egalitarian view is both harmful and contrary to Scripture . . . [advocating] husband as wimp . . . wife as usurper . . . men become unmasculine . . . women become unfeminine . . . ambivalence toward sex . . . moving contrary to nature (Romans 1:26)."[3]

One evangelical biblical scholar, Kevin Giles, has identified many expressions, such as "equal but different," that conceal an agenda: a gender hierarchy with men at the top.[4] "Complementarians" repeatedly affirm the equality of men and women while denying women equal opportunities for service. This is reminiscent of George Orwell's pigs' mantra: "All animals are equal, but some are more equal than others."

This book argues that men and women are equal not only before God but also in practice in the body of Christ—namely, in church life. We who affirm the equal rights and responsibilities of men and women do not deny God's creation of men and women with differences that complement one another. We celebrate those differences.

BIBLICAL WOMANHOOD

I use the term "biblical womanhood" for the idea promoted by the Council on Biblical Manhood and Womanhood that the Bible teaches God-ordained male leadership and female submission in the home and subordination in the church. Practically, this means that only men can hold leadership positions over men in the church and that wives bear a unique burden to submit to their husbands. But just because someone puts the word "biblical" before a concept does not make it biblical. I do not believe that the Bible actually teaches "biblical womanhood."

"Complementarians" say that taking leadership and being submissive are gender "roles" (a modern, non-biblical word, incorrectly used to justify *permanent* positions) established by God as "biblical manhood and womanhood." I use the term "biblical womanhood" in this book's title because "complementarians" use it to limit the roles of women. I also use it because this book focuses primarily on Bible passages about women in authority, and so focuses on biblical womanhood more than "biblical manhood."

PROCEDURE AND ACKNOWLEDGEMENTS

This book proceeds in biblical order, from Genesis to the Gospels and Acts, and ends with the epistles, where it addresses together the passages about husbands and wives in mutual submission. I begin most New Testament and some Old Testament sections with my own translation that to the best of my ability expresses the original meaning and closely reflects the original wording. Unless they are indented quotes, I put my translations and citations from other versions in quotation marks. NIV citations are in italics. Unless another source is identified, translations are my own. You are free to skip ahead to passages that concern you most.

Special thanks to Iveta Adams, Andrew Bartlett, Randy Colver, Kevin Giles, Vince Huffaker, Dick Kantzer, Douglas Knighton, and Brendan and Catherine Jones Payne for their keen editorial observations, and to www.linguistsoftware.com for the VaticanusLSU, OdysseaUBSU, NewJerusalemU, and TransitLSU fonts.

If you have more questions about the topic that this book does not answer, I encourage you to read some of the many other excellent biblical scholars and writers on this topic. Just some of those great writers include Beth Allison Barr, Michael Bird, Aimee Byrd, Manfred T. Brauch, Felicity Dale, Peter Davids, Eldon J. Epp, Gordon Fee, Kevin Giles, Rebecca Merrill Groothuis, Mimi Haddad, Richard Hess, Jamin Hübner, Carolyn James, Walter C. Kaiser, Scot McKnight, Ronald W. Pierce, Jackie Roese, G. J. A. Sitther, Aída Besançon Spencer, and Ben Witherington III. Some of their articles and many other fine resources are available for free download from the Christians for Biblical Equality website at https://www.cbeinternational.org.

NOTES

1. https://www.etsjets.org/files/documents/Chicago_Statement.pdf.
2. E.g. Wayne Grudem, *Evangelical Feminism & Biblical Truth* (Sisters, OR: Multnomah, 2004), 54.
3. Grudem, 52–55.
4. Kevin Giles, "The Genesis of Confusion: How 'Complementarians' Have Corrupted Communication," *Priscilla Papers* 29, 1 (2015): 22–29 at n. 42, online at https://www.cbeinternational.org/resource/article/priscilla-papers-academic-journal/genesis-confusion-how-complementarians-have, citing George W. Knight III, "Male and Female Related He Them," *Christianity Today* 20, no. 14 (April 9, 1976): 13–17.

One

CREATION AND FALL: GENESIS 1–3

Creation is the crucial starting point because it identifies God's intention in creating man and woman. It also shows how sin corrupted God's intention that men and women rule together over the earth, resulting in men ruling over women. The Bible as God revealed it, properly translated and interpreted, affirms the dominion of men and women over the rest of creation and that God gifts both men and women for leadership. Genesis affirms the equal rights and responsibilities of men and women, *not* male headship, as God's original design.

GENESIS 1–2:
THE CREATION OF MAN AND WOMAN

The Council on Biblical Manhood and Womanhood's Danvers Statement, prepared in 1987, asserts: "Adam's headship in marriage was established by God before the Fall."[1] Let's look at the actual words of Genesis to see if this is true.

Genesis 1 gives the big picture of the whole of creation. That story culminates in the creation of man and woman. It addresses man and woman equally. It affirms that humankind as male and female are created in God's image and likeness. God gives both man and woman the same blessing and the same dominion over the earth and all animals. Their equality is evident in the thirteen words that are plural in Hebrew, including Hebrew verbs that specify a plural subject, highlighted in bold below:

> **26** Then God said, "Let us make mankind in our image, in our likeness, so that **they** may **rule** over the fish in the sea and the birds in the sky, over the livestock and all the wild animals, and over all the creatures that move along the ground." **27** So God created mankind in his own image, in the image of God he created them;[2] **male and female** he created **them**. **28** God blessed **them** and said to **them**, "Be fruitful and **increase** in number; **fill** the earth and **subdue** it. **Rule** over the fish in the sea and the birds in the sky and over every living creature that moves on the ground." **29** Then God said, "I give **you** every seed-bearing plant on the face of the whole earth and every tree that has fruit with seed in it. They will be **yours** for food." **30** And it was so. . . . **31** and it was very good. (Gen. 1:26–31)

Genesis 1 does not teach any difference between the responsibilities or roles of men and women. To the contrary, it teaches that God:

- creates both male and female in God's image and likeness (1:26–27)
- gives both male and female rule over all the animals of the earth (1:26, 28)
- gives both male and female the same blessing and tells them together to be fruitful and increase in number, fill the earth, and subdue it (1:28), stating no distinction in roles

- speaks directly to both male and female (1:28–29 to "*them*," to "*you*" plural, twice)
- gives male and female together all plants for food (1:29 "*you*," "*yours*" plural)

Genesis 2 focuses specifically on the creation of man and woman. In contrast to the repeated affirmation "*It was good*" for every other stage of creation (Gen. 1:10, 12, 18, 21, 25, 31), God declares, "It is not good for the man to be alone; I will make a partner for him" (Gen. 2:18, cf. 20 NEB). Stop here and notice that this highlights the original purpose of woman: to be a friend and companion to man. Man does not need an assistant to remove thorns or thistles from the garden (see 3:18) or mend his clothes (see 2:25). He needs a friend and companion. God creates woman so the man will not be alone. Nothing in the creation narrative subordinates woman to man. The creation of woman is actually its climax.

The woman fulfills man's need for a partner corresponding to him (Gen. 2:18, 20). Many Bible versions describe the woman as "*a helper suitable for him.*" The Hebrew text, however, describes the woman as an *ezer kenegdo*, "a saving strength corresponding to him." The word *ezer* is often translated "*helper,*" which implies a subordinate or servant. Never in the Bible, however, does the word *ezer* require the meaning "*helper*" as in "servant." Rather, it suggests that the *ezer* is able to do something for another person which that person is not capable of doing. All nineteen other occurrences of *ezer* refer to a savior or deliverer. Sixteen refer to God as his people's rescuer, strength, or savior. For example:

> I'll name him Eliezer, because the God my father worshiped
> has saved me [been my *ezer*] from the king of Egypt.
> (Ex. 18:4 CEV)

> People of Israel, trust in the LORD!
>
> He is your strength [*ezer*] and shield. (Ps. 115:9 ERV)

> O Israel, if I destroy you, who can save you [be your *ezer*]?
> (Hos. 13:9 TLB)

The three other occurrences describe a military protector. The Bible has no instance where *ezer* clearly refers to an "assistant" or subordinate "*helper*." Nothing in Genesis 2 or any passage about God implies that either woman or God, as *ezer*, is subordinate to man. Rather, she is a "saving strength" without whom he cannot multiply.

The word that modifies *ezer* in Gen. 2:18, 20 is *kenegdo*. It is comprised of three parts: *ke* ("as") + *negd* ("in front of") + *o* ("him") and so conveys "as in front of him." Therefore, *ezer kenegdo*, is better translated "a saving strength corresponding to him." The Hebrew noun *nagid* is related to *negd*. *Nagid* means "the person in front." It identifies "the leader of Israel, appointed by Yahweh"[3] and describes Saul's, David's, and Solomon's rule over Israel in 1 Sam. 9:16; 10:1; 13:14, 25:30; 2 Sam. 6:21; 7:8; and 1 Kings 1:35. Therefore, like *ezer*, *kenegdo* indicates a superior or equal, not a subordinate. Nothing in the expression *ezer kenegdo* in Genesis 2 implies that God created woman as a subordinate helper for man. Quite the opposite, it highlights her strength as an equal partner with man designed to rescue him from being alone. She is his counterpart, his companion and friend who alongside him exercises dominion over the earth. She fulfills him so that together they can be fruitful and care for the earth.

Nothing in the Genesis 2 account of the creation of man and woman grants man priority in status or authority over woman.

Like the Genesis 1 account, it consistently emphasizes their equality. God makes woman from the man's rib, and the man recognizes, "*This is now bone of my bones and flesh of my flesh*" (2:23), because they literally share the same flesh and bone (2:21–23). John Chrysostom, the "golden mouthed" archbishop of Constantinople (AD 347–407), affirms that Eve "was not subjected as soon as she was made; nor, when He brought her to the man, did either she hear any such things from God, nor did the man say any such word to her: he said indeed that she was 'bone of his bone, and flesh of his flesh' (Gen. ii, 23); but of rule or subjection he no where [sic] made mention unto her."[4] "*Father and mother*" and "*man*" and "*wife*" are identified without hierarchical distinction (2:24). In marriage, they are "*united*" and "*one flesh*" (2:24). Both are naked and feel no shame; they share moral innocence (2:25). Genesis 1–2 consistently stresses man-woman equality.

GENESIS 1–2: ANSWERS TO OBJECTIONS

"God allowed Adam to define the woman, in keeping with Adam's headship."[5] Genesis 2:23's "sovereign act" of naming implies that man has authority over woman.

People who create something have authority over what they create, including naming rights. For example, when God says, "Let there be light" (Gen. 1:3) and "Let us make human beings in our image" (1:26 MSG), as creator, God has authority and naming rights. Similarly, parents have authority over and name the children they conceive. Simply naming something does not, however, give anyone authority over anything. Genesis 2:19–20 recounts the man's naming the animals:

So God formed out of the ground all the wild animals and all
the birds of heaven. He brought them to the man to see what
he would call them, and whatever the man called each living
creature, that was its name. Thus the man gave names to all
cattle, to the birds of heaven and to every wild animal; but for
the man himself no partner had yet been found. (NEB)

God as creator had the right to name all the creatures, but
God gave the man this honor. Genesis nowhere indicates that
the man's naming the animals gave him any more authority
over them than God gave to the woman. Genesis 1:26, 28, and 29
repeatedly state that God gave dominion over animals to both
man and woman with no indication of any distinction in their
authority.

Regarding the creation of woman, the man was totally passive; he created nothing. God made woman from one of the man's
ribs and the man slept through the whole thing (2:21). Sleeping
through the woman's creation did not give the man authority over
her or the right to name her.

When the Lord brought the woman to the man, he recognized his female counterpart and exclaimed with joy, "At last!
Bone of my bones and flesh of my flesh—she shall be called *ishah*
(woman), for she was taken out of *ish* (man)" (2:23). The name
"woman" (*ishah*) is merely the Hebrew word for "man" (*ish*) with
a feminine ending. Their corresponding names reinforce their
oneness of essence. "*Woman*" is not a proper name.

The naming formula in Genesis has three elements: the Kal
form of "call," the word for "name" (*shem*), and a specific name, as
in, "The man called his wife's name (*shem*) Eve" (Gen. 3:20; cf. 2:19;
4:17, 25, 26; 32:30). "Call" in Genesis 2:23 is Niphal, not Kal, and it
includes neither "name" (*shem*) nor a proper name.

"Man was created first. That implies that man has authority over woman."

Nowhere does Genesis indicate that because God created man first, man has authority over woman. Animals created on the fifth day are not given authority over animals created on the sixth day. Nor do any of them have authority over man and woman, who were created later.

Regarding humans, each reference to their authority is to their joint authority, not a hierarchy of authority. The creation of woman later is crucial to convey that the man recognized his need for a partner corresponding to him. Genesis says nothing about an "order of creation" in the sense of a hierarchy of authority, with authority given to the one created first.

In spite of the Near Eastern custom of giving preference to firstborn sons, at crucial junctures God *almost always subverts* this custom: God made his covenant with Isaac over Ishmael, blessed Jacob over Esau, Joseph over his older brothers, Ephraim over Manasseh, Perez over Zerah in the line of Christ, Moses over Aaron, David over his seven older brothers, and Solomon over Adonijah.

"But later in the Bible, in 1 Corinthians 11 and again in 1 Timothy 2, Paul talks about the creation of man and woman in Genesis in order to demonstrate the leadership role of men and the subordinate role of women."

Actually, he does not. Not at all. But that is skipping ahead too far. I will get to those verses later.

GENESIS 3: THE FALL

Genesis 3:1–5 narrates the conversation in which "the serpent," who "*was more crafty than any of the wild animals the Lord God had* made,"[6] addresses the woman (3:1, 5), "*God knows that when you eat from it your eyes will be opened, and you will be like God, knowing good and evil.*"

After this conversation, verse 6 states, "*When the woman saw that the fruit of the tree was good for food and pleasing to the eye, and also desirable for gaining wisdom, she took some and ate it. She also gave some to her husband, who was with her, and he ate it.*" The reason she ate the forbidden fruit reflects the serpent's deceptive words. It was "*desirable for gaining wisdom.*" The man's response to God, however, mentions nothing of the serpent's conversation with the woman. Unless Adam heard something that Genesis doesn't say he heard, his eating the forbidden fruit does not even rise to the level of deception—it is simply disobedience.

Because the woman disobeyed God's command, God addresses her directly in verse 13, "*What is this you have done?*" The woman responded, "*The serpent deceived me, and I ate.*" God cursed "the serpent," then God told the woman and the man the specific consequences of their disobedience.

Then God said to the woman, "I will cause you to have much trouble [or increase your pain] when you are pregnant [in child-bearing], and when you give birth to children, you will have great pain. You will greatly desire [the word implies a desire to control; 4:7] your husband, but he will rule over you" (Gen. 3:16 EXB).

The phrase "to (*el*) your husband [will be] your desire (*teshuqah*)" in Gen. 3:16c is rare. In English this may sound like romantic desire. But its meaning is evident from its closest parallel, Gen. 4:7, separated by only fourteen verses. The five words in Gen. 4:7b are in the identical order as those same words in Gen. 3:16c:

"to (*el*) your husband [will be] your desire (*teshuqah*), but (*ve*) he will rule (*mashal*) over (*be*) you," (Gen. 3:16c)

"To (el) you [is] his [sin's] desire (teshuqah), but (ve) you must rule (mashal[7]) over (be) him [sin]." (Gen. 4:7b regarding sin and Cain)

Sin desires Cain, which means that sin desires to control or manipulate Cain. Similarly, "Your desire will be for your husband" probably means "Your desire will be to control or manipulate your husband." The fall had transformed the relationship of Adam and Eve from sharing dominion over God's creation into a fierce power struggle, with each party trying to control the other.

All the other effects of the fall are clearly contrary to and distortions of God's intent in creation and all describe something new. It would be out of harmony with every other consequence of the fall to interpret the woman's "desire" as romantic or man's rule over woman as something good that should be fostered. Everything in 3:14–19 is disastrous news for the person addressed, and every other result of the fall for humankind is something people should try to overcome, such as pain in childbearing (through medical or relaxation techniques) and removal of thorns and thistles (through weeding). People should strive to overcome, rather than foster, the consequences of the fall, including the husband's rule over his wife and the wife's desire to rule over her husband. Pope John Paul II also argues that man's rule over women is a result of the fall that we should "overcome" because it disturbs our "fundamental equality."[8]

Finally, notice the equality of man and woman throughout this chapter. Together, they face temptation and disobey God's command (3:6). They both realize they are naked and sew coverings (3:7). Both hide from God (3:8), showing that they are both ashamed of their disobedience. Both pass the blame (3:12–13). God speaks directly to both, announcing specific consequences of their sin (3:9–13, 16–19). And in the end, both are personally responsible for their own disobedience.

GENESIS 3: ANSWERS TO OBJECTIONS

"Why does God call out to Adam, 'Where are you?' . . . Because, as the God-appointed head, Adam bore the primary responsibility to lead. . . . She usurped his headship."[9]

Genesis 3:13 states, *"Then the Lord God said to the woman, 'What is this you have done?' The woman said, 'The serpent deceived me, and I ate.'"* Clearly, then, the man does not speak for her. The Bible never explains why God calls the man first. Maybe it is simply because the man was the first one to be told, *"You must not eat from the tree of the knowledge of good and evil"* (2:17). Perhaps God questions the man first because the man was created first and has more experience with God and hence more reason to trust and obey God. Perhaps God speaks to the man, then to the woman, then to the serpent because only this order traces the sin back from the man to the woman to the serpent. The text then lists their consequences in the order of their actions: the serpent spoke to the woman, who gave the fruit to her husband, and he ate it. This order fits the narrative structure of Gen. 3:1–13 perfectly. Nothing in the text justifies reading into this detail of the story the idea that men should have authority over women.

"God created man to rule over woman. When God says, 'he shall rule over you,' he is talking only about 'harsh'[10] rule, not God-designed leadership."

Wayne Grudem should know that without evidence from Hebrew dictionaries, he should not say this "rule" is "harsh." He states two pages earlier[11] that he was wrong to assert without support from Hebrew dictionaries that another word from this same verse signifies an aggressive "desire to conquer."

Hebrew has many words for "rule," and some of them imply

bad rule or oppression. This one does not. The word here is by far the most common word for "rule" in the Hebrew Bible. For example, it occurs in these verses as well:

> The Israelites said to Gideon, "**Rule** over us—you, your son and
> your grandson—because you have saved us from the
> hand of Midian." (Judg. 8:22)

> for dominion belongs to the Lord
> and he **rules** over the nations. (Ps. 22:28)

Both major Hebrew dictionaries analyze every Old Testament instance of this word meaning rule and list no negative meaning for it. This word does not imply bad rule.

Furthermore, virtually all Bible versions translate this verb, like every other verb in God's predictions, as something that will happen in the future: "He **will** [or **shall**] *rule over you.*" Like all the other results of the fall, this is something new and contrary to God's original design for creation. This verb implies that prior to this, the man had not ruled over the woman. Genesis 3:16 does not specify oppressive rule. We should not foster what the fall initiated, namely men's rule over women, but rather God's originally intended mutual dominion by men and women together.

"Adam sinned by 'listening to his wife.' He abandoned his headship."[12]

Genesis 3:17 says that God curses the ground "*because you listened to your wife and ate fruit from the tree about which I commanded you, 'You must not eat from it.'*" God says this because Adam blames "*the woman you put here with me*" (3:12) for his eating the fruit. God rebukes Adam because he disobeyed God, blames the woman, and implicitly blames God for putting her there. God doesn't ask,

"Have you listened to your wife?" but "*Have you eaten from the tree that I commanded you not to eat from?*" (Gen. 3:11). Listening to his wife was a sin only because it entailed disobeying God.

NOTES

1. https://cbmw.org/about/danvers-statement/.
2. Hebrew singular, for "mankind," HALOT 2:14.
3. HALOT 2:668; cf. BDB 617.
4. NFPF[1] 12:150–51.
5. Raymond C. Ortlund, Jr., "Male-Female Equality and Male Headship: Genesis 1–3," in *Recovering Biblical Manhood and Womanhood: A Response to Evangelical Feminism*, ed. John Piper and Wayne Grudem (Wheaton, IL: Crossway, 1991), 95–112, at 103.
6. This distinguishes "the serpent," Satan (Rev. 20:2), from all the animals.
7. "Rule" in 3:16 and 4:7 are both Kal future singular masculine. The only difference in their grammatical form is the shift from the third person, "he," in 3:16 to the second person, "you," in 4:7.
8. Pope John Paul II, *On the Dignity and Vocation of Women: Mulieris Dignitatem* (Boston: Daughters of St. Paul, 1988), 24.
9. Ortlund, "Genesis 1–3," 107–9.
10. Grudem, *Evangelical Feminism*, 40.
11. Grudem, *Evangelical Feminism*, 38 n. 27.
12. Ortlund, "Genesis 1–3," 110.

Two

OLD TESTAMENT WOMEN
AND LEADERSHIP

The Old Testament says much more about women in leadership than this short book can cover, from people like Sheerah, daughter of Beriah, who "built Lower and Upper Beth Horon as well as Uzzen Sheerah" (1 Chron. 7:24) to Deborah, the only female leader of Israel in the book of Judges. Scripture's record of her rule was entirely positive for the people of God.

DEBORAH:
GOD'S CHOSEN LEADER

Deborah is one of the judges "*the Lord raised up*," judges who "*saved them out of the hands of their enemies*" (Judg. 2:16–18; cf. 4:9–10, 14, 24; 5:1–31). She is a prophet and the highest leader in Israel:

> Now Deborah, a prophet, the wife of Lappidoth, was leading Israel at
> that time. She held court under the Palm of Deborah between Ramah
> and Bethel in the hill country of Ephraim, and the Israelites went up
> to her to have their disputes decided. (Judg. 4:4–5)

Notice that there is no suggestion whatsoever in the text that there is anything amiss because this judge, Deborah, is a woman or that she has any obligation to defer to her husband. She is simply the leader of Israel, and people come to her for judgment.

Furthermore, she, a wife and mother (5:7), has authority to command Barak, Israel's military commander, "Go" (4:6, 14), which results in their successful defeat of Jabin's army. They work so well together, he as military commander and she as commander in chief, that Hebrews 11's celebration of heroes of the faith includes Barak:

> And what more shall I say? I do not have time to tell about Gideon, Barak, Samson and Jephthah, about David and Samuel and the prophets, who through faith conquered kingdoms, administered justice, and gained what was promised; who shut the mouths of lions, quenched the fury of the flames, and escaped the edge of the sword; whose weakness was turned to strength; and who became powerful in battle and routed foreign armies. (Heb. 11:32–34)

"I do not have time to tell about . . . the prophets" proves that there were other heroes. Since Deborah was a prophet and since 11:11 and 31 highlight other women, Sarah and Rahab, Barak's inclusion may imply Deborah because they worked together. After all, she "administered justice, and gained what was promised . . . and routed foreign armies." Her leadership blessed Israel:

> Then the land had peace forty years. (Judg. 5:31)

Deborah powerfully demonstrates God's blessing on female leadership.

DEBORAH: ANSWERS TO OBJECTIONS

"Deborah did not prophesy in public. . . . She did not exercise leadership over men as the other judges did."[1]

Judges 4:4–5 and 5:3, 15 flatly contradict both these denials:

> Deborah . . . was leading Israel at that time. She held court under the Palm of Deborah between Ramah and Bethel in the hill country of Ephraim, and the Israelites went up to her to have their disputes decided . . . "Hear this, you kings! Listen, you rulers! I, even I, will sing to the Lord . . . The princes of Issachar were with Deborah . . ."

"During this time, Israel was enslaved after worshipping false gods, and the people were completely corrupt. No man could be found to lead, so Deborah became the leader. Since all the other judges in the Bible were men, God clearly prefers men to lead."

The idea that God could not find a man to lead may at first glance appear plausible. After all, many Old Testament male leaders of God's people were reluctant at first. God asked Moses and Gideon, the judge immediately after Deborah, to lead Israel, and they both came up with excuse after excuse. However, God was willing and able to use "shock and awe" to persuade both of them to become Israel's leaders. Moses finally agreed only after God performed many signs and wonders and allowed him to take his brother Aaron along to do the speaking. Similarly, Gideon ultimately agreed after extensive negotiations with God and witnessing signs and wonders. We know that Barak was a willing leader who only needed a little prompting to lead his troops into battle—surely God could have convinced Barak to be Israel's judge if God had wanted to. Deborah was the leader of Israel because God chose her to lead Israel, not because

God tried to get a male leader but failed and had to "settle" for a woman.

"Because of Israel's awful circumstances, we should not take Deborah's leadership as a normal example. It was a one-time exception for exceptional times."

Actually, the times were not that exceptional. Yes, Israel had been enslaved by the Canaanites. But Israel had been enslaved before. Just think about the Egyptian captivity. Then Israel was in the desert for forty years (Ex. 16:35). Israel had already been enslaved two other times in Judges before Deborah, and they would be enslaved many other times after Deborah. Following the judges, there were a few good kings and many awful kings. There was nothing particularly exceptional about the time when Deborah was chosen by God to lead Israel. If God had desired only men in leadership, God could have made this happen and could have clearly revealed this in Scripture. But God did not.

"Every other judge before and after Deborah was 'raised up' by God to deliver Israel militarily from their enemies. Deborah 'has no military function.'[2] Barak was the military leader who delivered Israel, not Deborah."

Judges 4:3–7 identifies Deborah as the answer to the Israelites prayer for deliverance from commander Sisera's cruel oppression. In any event, which is easier: (1) to lead your troops into a single battle when God has already guaranteed victory and actually drawn up the battle plans, or (2) to lead a sinful, rebellious nation into forty years of peace? Give Barak credit for trusting Deborah with his life and the lives of his men and going into battle. Deborah, however, is the exceptional leader here.

"Because Barak asked Deborah (a woman) to accompany him into battle, he was denied the honor of killing the commander of the enemy forces—the honor went to a woman instead. This demonstrates that it was a sign of weakness for him to ask a woman to join him. He should have just 'been a man' and led his troops by himself."

I agree that when Deborah tells Barak that God wants him to lead his troops into battle, the best response would have been for Barak to go directly without question. Had he done that, Judg. 4:9 seems to imply that he would have been able to kill Sisera himself and would have been honored for that. However, that honor goes instead to Jael, the wife of Heber (Judg. 4:21). But in the end, because Barak obeys Deborah, Barak's army is successful, Israel is freed, Deborah's song praises Barak (Judg. 5:12), and Barak's name is in Hebrews 11's legion of honor. So, the "honor" Barak loses due to his initial demand that Deborah accompany him in battle—which shows how highly he and his troops respected Deborah—is tiny in comparison to the larger honor God gives him because he obeys her command. This teaches that we should obey God's messengers, whether men or women.

"Given Israel's decrepit spiritual state at the time, we should not understand Judges as illustrating God's ideal—God was simply working with the people he had."

Yes, the Israelites repeatedly disobeyed God's judges. However, nothing in the description of judge Deborah implies that she was not God's choice or was somehow second best.

KINGS AND PRIESTS: MALE ONLY?

Previous objections assumed that God prefers male leaders. Consider, however, the two major types of leaders in the Old

Testament: kings and priests. Even though there are not that many judges, the book of Judges does, indeed, reflect God's ideal leadership structure, with judges guiding Israel under God, their true king. (God is supposed to be our king; we are not meant to have human kings.) But the people revolt and demand a king, so God relents, as 1 Samuel records:

> And the Lord told him [Samuel]: "Listen to all that the people are saying to you; it is not you they have rejected, but they have rejected me as their king. As they have done from the day I brought them up out of Egypt until this day, forsaking me and serving other gods, so they are doing to you. Now listen to them; but warn them solemnly and let them know what the king who will reign over them will claim as his rights." (1 Sam. 8:7–9)

Originally, God's people were just supposed to live according to the covenant. God raised up judges to deliver Israel and put them back on the right path. God alone should be king.

Scripture criticizes every male king of Israel or Judah. Athaliah (a queen who "ruled the land" for six years, 2 Kings 11:1–3; 2 Chron. 22:10–12) and Jezebel were also wicked, but neither they nor any other women who led Israel are criticized in Scripture on the grounds that a woman should not rule.

Queen Esther used her influence to save the Jews from annihilation (Est. 7:1–10; 9:1–32). The Bible's portrayal of the Queen of Sheba (1 Kings 10:1–13; 2 Chron. 9:1–12) and the Queen of Chaldea (Dan. 5:10–12) is purely positive. English has completely different words for "king" and "queen." This makes it appear that kings are distinct from queens. However, in Hebrew and other Semitic languages, both the word for "king" and the word for "queen" are noun forms of the verb "to rule" (malak). The word for "queen," *malkah*, is the feminine form of the word for "king." Furthermore, these women are the only three people with the title derived from "rule" (whether "king" or "queen") whom the Bible portrays as entirely positive with no hint of criticism. So it would be a mistake to think that male kings in the Bible prove that God desires or praises only male leadership.

Furthermore, the records of the kings of Judah always note or name the queen mothers (cf. Jer. 13:18; 29:2; 2 Kings 24:15). They include Bathsheba (1 Kings 2:17–19), Maacah (1 Kings 15:2, 10, 13), and Nehushta (2 Kings 24:8).

What about priests? God did assign the priesthood to Aaron and his sons (Num. 18:1–7). The Bible does not give a reason for this, but Deut. 23:17 may imply one: "None of the daughters of Israel shall be a temple prostitute" (NRSV). Priestesses were closely associated with prostitutes and cultic sexual rites in the surrounding heathen cults. God repeatedly prohibited his people from giving the appearance of following the immoral practices of the surrounding nations. To have women priests would have given that appearance. First Samuel 2:22 confirms the importance of this in practice.

In any event, we know that the limitation of the priesthood to Aaron's sons was not God's long-term plan because God explicitly states that the entire people of Israel should be "*a kingdom of priests and a holy nation*":

> Then Moses went up to God, and the Lord called to him from the mountain and said, "This is what you are to say to the descendants of Jacob and what you are to tell the people of Israel: 'You yourselves have seen what I did to Egypt, and how I carried you on eagles' wings and brought you to myself. Now if you obey me fully and keep my covenant, then out of all nations you will be my treasured possession.

> Although the whole earth is mine, you will be for me a kingdom of
> priests and a holy nation.' These are the words you are to speak to
> the Israelites." (Ex. 19:3–6)

Isaiah 61:6 predicts a future when all God's people "*will be
called priests of the Lord, you will be named ministers of our God.*"

And ultimately, God brought about the priesthood of all his
people in the New Testament church:

> But you are a chosen people, a royal priesthood, a holy nation, God's
> special possession, that you may declare the praises of him who called
> you out of darkness into his wonderful light. (1 Pet. 2:9)

Although God established male priests of the sons of Aaron,
Jesus is now our high priest and male and female believers are all
priests with a direct connection to God.

PROVERBS 31: AN EXCELLENT WIFE

The most extensive Bible passage on the position of a wife and
her activities is the description of an excellent wife in Proverbs
31:10–31:

> A wife of noble character who can find?
> She is worth far more than rubies.
> Her husband has full confidence in her
> and lacks nothing of value.
> She brings him good, not harm,
> all the days of her life.
> She selects wool and flax
> and works with eager hands.

She is like the merchant ships,

    bringing her food from afar.

She gets up while it is still night;

    she provides food for her family

    and portions for her female servants.

She considers a field and buys it;

    out of her earnings she plants a vineyard.

She sets about her work vigorously;

    her arms are strong for her tasks.

She sees that her trading is profitable,

    and her lamp does not go out at night.

In her hand she holds the distaff

    and grasps the spindle with her fingers.

She opens her arms to the poor

    and extends her hands to the needy.

When it snows, she has no fear for her household;

    for all of them are clothed in scarlet.

She makes coverings for her bed;

    she is clothed in fine linen and purple.

Her husband is respected at the city gate,

    where he takes his seat among the elders of the land.

She makes linen garments and sells them,

    and supplies the merchants with sashes.

She is clothed with strength and dignity;

    she can laugh at the days to come.

She speaks with wisdom,

    and faithful instruction is on her tongue.

She watches over the affairs of her household

    and does not eat the bread of idleness.

Her children arise and call her blessed;

    her husband also, and he praises her:

"Many women do noble things,
    but you surpass them all."
Charm is deceptive, and beauty is fleeting;
    but a woman who fears the Lord is to be praised.
Honor her for all that her hands have done,
    and let her works bring her praise at the city gate.

So what characterizes this idealized *"wife of noble character"*?
She is an efficient executive with a well-ordered domestic staff.
She deals in real estate, runs a clothing business, and cares for the
poor as well as her own household. She has her own earnings. She
appears to be the primary income earner in the family. She is also
a wise and kind teacher. How does this line up with hierarchical
gender roles?

WOMEN AS PROPHETS

We have discussed the prophet Deborah, but the Old Testament
also praises many other women—including wives and mothers—
who exercised leadership over men. It describes God's blessing on
women in leadership with no hint that their gender should dis-
qualify them. The prophet Miriam is sent by God *"to lead"* Israel:

I brought you up out of Egypt
    and redeemed you from the land of slavery.
I sent Moses to lead you,
    also Aaron and Miriam.
        (Mic. 6:4, cf. Ex. 15:20; Isa. 8:3; Neh. 6:14)

Priests consult the prophet Huldah when they find the lost
book of the law. They submit to her spiritual leadership. Israel's

leaders, including the king, the elders, the prophets, and the people, accept her word as divinely revealed (2 Kings 22:14–23:3; 2 Chron. 34:22–32). Israel's male leadership obeys God's word spoken through Huldah. She sparks what is probably the greatest revival in the history of Israel (2 Kings 22:14–23:25; 2 Chron. 34:29–35:19).

Not one Old Testament text says that God permitted women to hold such political or religious authority over men only because of special circumstances. Nor do these texts describe those women as exceptions to a scriptural principle. Scripture nowhere criticizes them or any other woman leader of Israel on the grounds that women should not have authority over men. Instead, Scripture presents women in religious and political leadership as normal in the comparatively few cases it records. Some are explicitly stated to have been raised up by God and blessed.

Indeed, the Old Testament teaches that God intends women to prophesy. Moses desired that *"all the Lord's people were prophets"*:

> A young man ran and told Moses, "Eldad and Medad are prophesying in the camp." Joshua son of Nun, who had been Moses' aide since youth, spoke up and said, "Moses, my lord, stop them!" But Moses replied, "Are you jealous for my sake? I wish that all the Lord's people were prophets and that the Lord would put his Spirit on them!" (Num. 11:27–29)

Later on, Joel 2:28–29 echoes that desire:

> And afterward,
>> I will pour out my Spirit on all people.
> Your sons and daughters will prophesy,
>> your old men will dream dreams,
>> your young men will see visions.

> Even on my servants, both men and women,
>> I will pour out my Spirit in those days.

And as you know, this wonderful promise is fulfilled at Pentecost:

> Then Peter stood up with the Eleven, raised his voice and addressed the crowd: "Fellow Jews and all of you who live in Jerusalem, let me explain this to you; listen carefully to what I say. These people are not drunk, as you suppose. It's only nine in the morning! No, this is what was spoken by the prophet Joel:
>
>> "'In the last days, God says,
>>> I will pour out my Spirit on all people.
>> Your sons and daughters will prophesy,
>>> your young men will see visions,
>>> your old men will dream dreams.
>> Even on my servants, both men and women,
>>> I will pour out my Spirit in those days,
>>> and they will prophesy.
>> I will show wonders in the heavens above
>>> and signs on the earth below,
>>> blood and fire and billows of smoke.
>> The sun will be turned to darkness
>>> and the moon to blood
>>> before the coming of the great and glorious day of the Lord.
>> And everyone who calls
>>> on the name of the Lord will be saved.'" (Acts 2:14–21)

Finally, God uses women in the greatest of all prophetic ministries: speaking key portions of inspired Scripture. These include the songs of Miriam (Ex. 15:21) and Deborah (Judg. 5:2–31), Hannah's prayer (1 Sam. 2:1–10), Abigail's prophecy (1 Sam. 25:28–31), and Proverbs 31, the "*inspired utterance*" of King Lemuel's mother (Prov. 31:1). Peeking ahead into the New Testament, God continues to speak through women in this way through the Song of Elizabeth (Luke 1:25, 42–45) and Mary's Magnificat, the first New Testament exposition of Scripture (Luke 1:46–55).

The Old Testament, therefore, clearly affirms that God appointed women to both secular and sacred leadership over men.

NOTES

1. Thomas R. Schreiner, "The Valuable Ministries of Women in the Context of Male Leadership: A Survey of Old and New Testament Examples and Teaching," in *Recovering Biblical Manhood*, 209–32, at 216.
2. Schreiner, "Male Leadership," 216.

Three

WOMEN IN MINISTRY FROM THE GOSPELS THROUGH ROMANS 16

JESUS AND WOMEN

Since Jesus is our Lord, understanding how he treats women is crucial. His teaching and behavior should guide our faith and practice. Any view of women that does not give them the respect that Jesus does is not a truly Christian view. In all his words and deeds, Jesus leaves us an example to treat women as equals with men, never subordinated or restricted in role.

> For whoever does the will of my Father in heaven is my brother and sister and mother.[1] (Matt. 12:50)

Jesus's treatment of women and men as equals defies the judicial, cultural, and religious customs of his day.

In judicial matters, women's rights were limited in many ways, including adultery and divorce. Jesus, however, treats men and women equally. For example, even though in general, first-century Palestinian Jewish women could not divorce their husbands, Jesus uses symmetrical wording to emphasize the equal responsibilities of husbands and wives regarding divorce.

> He answered, "Anyone who divorces his wife and marries another woman commits adultery against her. And if she divorces her husband and marries another man, she commits adultery." (Mark 10:11–12)

Also in this passage and Matt. 19:9, Jesus labels the husband "an adulterer" even though in the Greco-Roman world, a man, unlike a woman, "committed adultery only by sexual relationships with a married woman."[2] This is such a controversial teaching that the disciples had difficulty accepting it:

> The disciples said to him, "If this is the situation between a husband and wife, it is better not to marry." (Matt. 19:10)

Even though women typically were not permitted as legal witnesses, Jesus states, "*The Queen of the South will rise at the judgment with the people of this generation and condemn them*" (Luke 11:31; Matt. 12:42).

It was culturally "unheard of and considered scandalous in Jewish circles"[3] for Jesus to welcome the support of women who left their homes and families to travel with him and other disciples (e.g. Luke 8:1–3).

In a culture that regarded women as intellectually and morally inferior to men, Jesus respects women's intelligence and spiritual capacity, as is evident in the great spiritual truths he teaches to women such as the Samaritan woman and Martha:

"God is spirit, and his worshipers must worship in the Spirit and in truth." The woman said, "I know that Messiah" (called Christ) "is coming. When he comes, he will explain everything to us."

Then Jesus declared, "I, the one speaking to you—I am he." (John 4:24–26)

Jesus said to her, "I am the resurrection and the life. The one who believes in me will live, even though they die; and whoever lives by believing in me will never die." (John 11:25–26)

In a culture that frowned upon the religious education of women,[4] Jesus encourages women to be his disciples. For example, when Mary sits *"at the Lord's feet listening to what he said"* (Luke 10:39), she takes the posture and position of a disciple. When Martha tells Jesus that she wants her sister Mary to stop learning at Jesus's feet as a disciple and come help her out, Jesus replies: *"Mary has chosen what is better, and it will not be taken away from her"* (Luke 10:42). It is generally agreed that disciples in Jesus's day were trained to carry on a rabbi's teachings, typically becoming teachers themselves.[5] Other rabbis taught only male disciples, but Jesus teaches both men and women disciples. This implies that Jesus wants women as well as men to teach his message.

Furthermore, Jesus teaches that resurrected people *"are equal to angels and are sons of God"* (Luke 20:36 RSV), making no distinction between male and female.

But does Jesus's choice of only men for the original twelve apostles, who had revered leadership positions in the early church, mean that he thereby excludes women from church leadership? No. His choice of the twelve apostles does not logically exclude women from church leadership any more than his choice of free Jews for the twelve apostles excludes gentiles or slaves from church leadership. In any event, two of the most influential early church leaders, James the brother of Jesus (Acts 15:13; Gal. 1:19) and Paul, were not among the Twelve. But they were still apostles, as was the woman Junia, whom Paul calls "*outstanding among the apostles*" (Rom. 16:7, see below, pp. 36–38, 45).

Since apostles other than the Twelve, including the apostle Junia, held church leadership positions, it is wrong to conclude from the gender of the Twelve that we should exclude women from church leadership.

So, then, why does Jesus choose all men and no women for the original twelve apostles? Although the New Testament does not explain his reasons, Jesus probably chooses men for two reasons: to avoid scandal and to symbolize the "new Israel." If Jesus had regularly included women in gatherings at night, especially in the wilderness or in places such as the garden of Gethsemane, this would have raised moral suspicions not only about Jesus, but also about the Twelve, on whose integrity the church would depend. When Jesus does meet with women, it is not in secret. Others are present or nearby, and Jesus tells these women to tell others about their meeting, as he does with the Samaritan woman and his resurrection appearance to Mary Magdalene (John 4:7–30; 20:1–18).[6] Furthermore, Jesus's appointment of twelve Jewish free men parallels the twelve sons of Israel and reinforces the symbolism of the church as the "new Israel" (Matt. 19:28; Luke 22:30; Rev. 21:12–14).

Jesus encourages women to proclaim the gospel to men. The first Christian missionary is a Samaritan woman: "*Many of the Samaritans from that town believed in him because of the woman's testimony*" (John 4:39; cf. 28–42). Also, the first person the resurrected Christ seeks out and commissions to announce the gospel of his resurrection and his coming ascension to God the Father is

Mary Magdalene (John 20:14–18). Since "apostle" means "one sent with a mission," it is appropriate to say that Christ appoints her an apostle to the apostles. Jesus Christ redefines leadership as humble servant-leadership (e.g., John 13:1–17). Servant-leadership is just as appropriate for women as men.

Jesus is crucially important for our theology of man and woman. Since Christ treats women as equal to men, respects their intelligence to handle even the deepest truths, teaches Mary as a disciple and the Samaritan woman who became the first evangelist, and commissions Mary Magdalene to announce his resurrection to the disciples, any theology of women that does not do similarly is not Christian.

ACTS 4: ANANIAS AND SAPPHIRA

The story of Ananias and Sapphira has interesting implications for gender equality. Acts explains that the Holy Spirit fills and empowers believers. This signals the beginning of the transformed Christian community:

> After they prayed, the place where they were meeting was shaken. And they were all filled with the Holy Spirit and spoke the word of God boldly.
>
> All the believers were one in heart and mind. No one claimed that any of their possessions was their own, but they shared everything they had. With great power the apostles continued to testify to the resurrection of the Lord Jesus. And God's grace was so powerfully at work in them all that there were no needy persons among them. For from time to time those who owned land or houses sold them, brought the money from the sales and put it at the apostles' feet, and it was distributed to anyone who had need.

> *Joseph, a Levite from Cyprus, whom the apostles called Barnabas (which means "son of encouragement"), sold a field he owned and brought the money and put it at the apostles' feet. (Acts 4:31–37)*

The text continues with a troubling story:

> *Now a man named Ananias, together with his wife Sapphira, also sold a piece of property. With his wife's full knowledge he kept back part of the money for himself, but brought the rest and put it at the apostles' feet.*
>
> *Then Peter said, "Ananias, how is it that Satan has so filled your heart that you have lied to the Holy Spirit and have kept for yourself some of the money you received for the land? Didn't it belong to you before it was sold? And after it was sold, wasn't the money at your disposal? What made you think of doing such a thing? You have not lied just to human beings but to God."*
>
> *When Ananias heard this, he fell down and died. And great fear seized all who heard what had happened. Then some young men came forward, wrapped up his body, and carried him out and buried him. (Acts 5:1–6)*

Ananias brings in the offering and lies about his gift, so his guilt is obvious. What about Sapphira? See what happens when Peter interviews her without her husband present:

> *About three hours later his wife came in, not knowing what had happened. Peter asked her, "Tell me, is this the price you and Ananias got for the land?"*
>
> *"Yes," she said, "that is the price."*
>
> *Peter said to her, "How could you conspire to test the Spirit of the Lord? Listen! The feet of the men who buried your husband are at the door, and they will carry you out also."*

> At that moment she fell down at his feet and died. Then the
> young men came in and, finding her dead, carried her out and buried
> her beside her husband. (Acts 5:7–10)

Judging from her dead body, she undoubtedly gave the wrong answer. I think it is safe to say that the right answer was to tell the truth, even if that got her husband into trouble.

She and her husband acted together. If God had intended the husband to be the "leader of the household" with authority to command his wife's obedience, then Ananias should have borne primary responsibility for the deception. If wives have a moral obligation to yield to their husbands, then she gives the right answer—that is, she affirms what her husband said. Indeed, if Ananias had any leadership or authority over her whatsoever, then her guilt should have been less. God, however, judges her to be completely and individually responsible for her actions, independent of her husband.[7] Consequently, she suffers the exact same punishment. This account of God's judgment contradicts the idea that a wife must obey or defend her husband and that a husband has authority to command his wife's obedience in analogous situations.

ROMANS 16: SEVEN WOMEN CHURCH LEADERS, INCLUDING DEACON PHOEBE AND THE APOSTLE JUNIA

The first person Paul acknowledges in Rom. 16:1–2 is Phoebe:

> I commend to you our sister Phoebe, who holds the office of
> deacon of the church in Cenchreae. Welcome her in the Lord as
> worthy of God's holy people, and help her in whatever matter

she may need your help, for she herself has been a leader of many, including myself.

The first thing to note is that the word "deacon" in Greek is *diakonos*, which is the same word used for "deacons" in Phil. 1:1 and 1 Tim. 3:8 and 12. In each of those cases the "deacons" were involved in church leadership roughly comparable to what we today call "ministers," as the NIV translates this word in Col. 1:7 and 1 Tim. 4:6. In some Bible versions, this word is translated "servant" here where it applies to a woman, and "deacon" elsewhere when it applies to men. But churches then didn't have "servants," and since this identifies Phoebe's position in the church in Cenchreae, "deacon" is correct, or to convey the meaning with its closest equivalent in English, "minister."

Second, the Greek states, "Phoebe, who is deacon of the church in Cenchreae." "Who is" makes it "very much more natural . . . to understand it as referring to a definite office."[8]

Third, Paul tells the Romans, "Welcome her" because he chose Phoebe to deliver his letter to the Roman churches. As Paul's trusted representative, she would have read it to them and would have answered any theological questions they might have asked. It is significant that Paul entrusted a woman to deliver and explain Romans, his most theologically comprehensive letter.

Fourth, Paul identifies Phoebe as a "leader [*prostatis*] of many." The NIV's "*benefactor*" is probably not the best translation because the New Testament consistently uses a different word for "benefactor," *euergetēs*, meaning "one who does good." Secular usage indicates that benefactors preferred the designation *euergetēs*, because it highlights generosity rather than power.

Prostatis can also, like the Latin *patrona* ("patroness"), denote the legal representative of strangers and their protector; for as aliens they were deprived of civil rights. This meaning does not fit Rom. 16:2, however, since "Phoebe cannot have stood in this relation to Paul since he was born free, Acts 22:28."[9] Furthermore, Paul's self-support (Acts 18:3; 1 Cor. 4:11–13; 9:1–27; 1 Thess. 2:9; 4:11–12) is incongruent with Phoebe being his patron.

Prostatis comes from the verb *proistēmi*, "to exercise a position of leadership." It combines the Greek words for "in rank before" and "standing," and so emphasizes the respect she should be given. This is the feminine form of the word for the "president" of a society, including synagogues. Every other New Testament word that combines these two words, "in rank before" and "standing," and has a meaning that fits Rom. 16:2, is about leaders. In these examples, this word is bold:

- If it [one's gift] is **leadership** . . . govern diligently. (Rom. 12:8 NIV 1973)
- Respect those **who** . . . **are over you** in the Lord. (1 Thess. 5:12 RSV)
- *The elders **who direct the affairs of the church** well are worthy of double honor.* (1 Tim. 5:17)
- Church officials must **be in control** of their own families. (1 Tim. 3:4 CEV; cf. 3:5, 12)

Even Charles Ryrie, who taught that woman's role in church is "not a leading one," acknowledged that *prostatis* "includes some kind of leadership."[10]

Furthermore, Paul acknowledges that Phoebe not only was "a **leader** of many," but "including myself" (Rom. 16:2). This implies that Paul submitted to her leadership, presumably when he was in the church in Cenchreae. Paul practiced the mutual submission he commands in Eph. 5:21. Paul's description of Phoebe would have encouraged those hearing this letter to value and respect her as a reliable resource regarding its meaning and significance.

In the final greetings of Romans, Paul repeatedly affirms male–female equality by identifying women as laboring alongside men in ministry. In Romans 16, Paul identifies the names and Christian ministries of ten people. Seven of these ten are women! Not only that, all four of the people Paul praises as "hard workers" are women. In addition to Phoebe, Paul identifies (in bold type):

- "Greet **Prisca** and Aquila, my coworkers in Christ Jesus, who risked their own lives for mine. Not only I but all the churches among the Gentiles give thanks to them. Also greet the church that meets in their house" (Rom. 16:3–5). Paul uses the respectful form of her name, not the diminutive form Priscilla, and names her before her husband, contrary to Greek convention. This must not have been required by her social status because 1 Cor. 16:19 and Acts 18:2, which are not about their ministry, list Aquila's name first. Consequently, Prisca's being listed first indicates her prominence as a coworker.
- "Greet **Mary**, who worked very hard in ministry[11] [*polla kopiaō*] among you." (16:6)
- "Greet Andronicus and **Junia**, my compatriots and fellow prisoners. They are outstanding among the apostles and also were in Christ before I was." (16:7) Even John Chrysostom (ca. AD 344–407), who typically disparages women in church leadership, confirms that Junia was an apostle: "Even to be an apostle is great, but also to be prominent among them [*en toutois episēmous*]—consider how wonderful a song of honor that is. For they were prominent because of their works, because of their successes. Glory be!

How great the wisdom of this woman that she was even deemed worthy of the apostle's title."[12]

- "Greet **Tryphaena** and **Tryphosa**, women who work hard [*kopiaō*] in the Lord." (16:12)
- "Greet my beloved **Persis**, another woman who has worked very hard [*polla kopiaō*] in the Lord." (16:12)

The significance of those who "*labor*" and "*work hard*" in the church becomes obvious in the use of these words elsewhere in Paul's letters. Paul tells believers to submit themselves to all co-laborers in Christ (without regard to gender):

> You know that the household of Stephanas were the first converts in Achaia, and they have devoted themselves to the service of the Lord's people. I urge you, brothers and sisters, to submit to such people and to everyone who joins in the work and labors [*kopiaō*] at it. (1 Cor. 16:15–16)

> Now we ask you, brothers and sisters, to acknowledge those who work hard [*kopiaō*] among you, who care for you in the Lord and who admonish you. Hold them in the highest regard in love because of their work. (1 Thess. 5:12–13)

It cannot be stressed enough that Paul lists these seven women not simply as *believers*, but as *ministry leaders*. He greets many believers in this passage, but describes as ministry leaders only ten people, and seven of them are women. The three men are Aquila, Andronicus, and Urbanus. The first two are listed with their wives. This highlights their shared authority. Paul's affirmation by name of such a high proportion of women leaders is unparalleled in the entire history of ancient Greek literature and indicates a level of female leadership in the early church exceptional for that culture.

Paul also affirms the coworkers Euodia and Syntyche (Phil. 4:2–3), and Lydia (Acts 16:14–15) and Nympha (Col. 4:15), in whose homes believers met (as also John Mark's mother Mary, Acts 12:12).

NOTES

1. No manuscript adds "and father," even though that would complete the nuclear family. This suggests that Jesus, just like Matthew (see Matt. 1:18–21) and Mark (Mark 3:35), understood that he was born of a virgin. See below, p. 174.

2. NIDNTT 2:582; TDNT 4:732, "Unconditional fidelity is demanded of the wife alone. The married man is not forbidden to have intercourse with an unmarried woman."

3. Ben Witherington III, *Women and the Genesis of Christianity* (Cambridge: Cambridge University Press, 1990), 110, noting that this "is unlikely to have been invented by a Christian community."

4. E.g. m. Soṭah 3.4, b. Soṭah 21b, b. Ber. 17a, y. Soṭah 3.4 (VII.D).

5. E.g. 2 Tim. 2:2; Heb. 5:12; and b. Qidd. 29a–b, "whoever is commanded to study is commanded to teach."

6. Cf. John 4:16 "*Go, call your husband and come back.*" There is enough light for Mary "*to look into the tomb*" and to see "*two angels in white*" (John 20:11, 12). Furthermore, Jesus says, "*Do not hold on to me*" (John 20:17).

7. God held Eve responsible, too. The Danvers Statement helpfully says: "In all of life Christ is the supreme authority and guide for men and women, so that no earthly submission-domestic, religious, or civil-ever implies a mandate to follow a human authority into sin (Dan 3:10-18; Acts 4:19-20; 5:27-29; 1 Pet 3:1-2)."

8. C. E. B. Cranfield, *A Critical and Exegetical Commentary on the Epistle to the Romans*, ICC (Edinburgh: T&T Clark, 1979), 2:781.

9. C. K. Barrett, *The Epistle to the Romans* (London: A. & C. Black, 1957), 283.

10. Charles C. Ryrie, *The Role of Women in the Church* (Chicago: Moody Press, 1958), 140 and 88.

11. As in Rom. 16:12; 1 Cor. 15:10, 58; Gal. 4:11–13; Phil. 2:16; Col. 1:28–29; 1 Tim. 4:10–11; 5:17.

12. Chrysostom, *In ep. ad Romanos* 31, 2 (PG 60:669–70). Translation from Eldon Jay Epp, *Junia: The First Woman Apostle* (Minneapolis: Fortress, 2005), 79.

Four

GENDER EQUALITY IN MARRIAGE AND SPIRITUAL GIFTS

1 Corinthians 7–10, 12

1 CORINTHIANS 7: HUSBAND–WIFE EQUALITY

Before we get to the "tough" passages, here is an easy one: 1 Corinthians 7. This chapter, Paul's longest and most detailed treatment of marriage, is simply stunning. Here, Paul affirms many rights and responsibilities of husbands and wives regarding eleven issues related to marriage. These issues include sexual relations, divorce, singleness, and sanctification. Throughout this passage, Paul addresses men and women as equals. His wording is symmetrically balanced to emphasize this equality. Regarding each issue, Paul affirms that husbands and wives have equal rights and responsibilities.

The first four issues concern sexual relations:

But because of cases of sexual immorality, each husband should have sexual relations with his own wife, and each wife should have sexual relations with her own husband. (7:2)

The husband must give to his wife what he owes her, and in exactly the same way the wife to her husband. (7:3)

The wife does not have authority over her own body, but her husband does. In exactly the same way, the husband does not have authority over his own body, but his wife does. (7:4)

Do not deprive each other sexually except by harmonious agreement for an appropriate time, so that you may devote yourselves to prayer. Then come together again. (7:5)

The next five issues concern divorce and remarriage, including the sanctification of an unbelieving spouse:

To those who are married I instruct—not I, but the Lord—a wife must not divorce, but if she does divorce, she must remain unmarried or be reconciled to her husband, and a husband must not divorce his wife. (7:10–11)

To the rest I say—I, not the Lord—if any brother has an unbelieving wife, and she is willing to live with him, he must not divorce her. And if any woman has an unbelieving husband, and he is willing to live with her, she must not divorce her husband. (7:12–13)

For the unbelieving husband is being made holy because of his wife, and the unbelieving wife is being made holy because of her husband. Otherwise your children would be unclean, but as it is, they are holy. (7:14)

But if the unbelieving spouse divorces, let that spouse divorce.

The brother or sister is not bound in such cases. God has called you, instead, to live in peace. (7:15)

How do you know, wife, that you will save your husband? Or, how do you know, husband, that you will save your wife? (7:16)

The final two issues concern motivations for men and women to get married or to stay single. For either gender, the advice is the same:

But if you do marry, you have not sinned; and if a virgin marries, she has not sinned. (7:28)

An unmarried man is concerned about the Lord's affairs—how he can please the Lord. But a married man is concerned about the affairs of this world—how he can please his wife—and his interests are divided. An unmarried woman or virgin is concerned about the Lord's affairs: Her aim is to be devoted to the Lord in both body and spirit. But a married woman is concerned about the affairs of this world—how she can please her husband. (7:32–34)

In summary, Paul encourages men and women to stay single so they may be more devoted to God's work. However, Paul also blesses those who desire to get married and describes how a Christian marriage should operate. Paul does not describe a hierarchy of any sort within the marriage, nor does he give either person the final word or veto power. Rather, he clearly treats husband and wife as equal and emphasizes their ministry. Particularly striking, especially for the Hellenistic culture of Paul's day, is 7:4, "The husband does not have authority over his own body, but his wife does." There is no hint of the husband having headship.

If Paul had intended the husband to be "head" of the wife in the sense of having authority over her or if this were central to Paul's view of marriage, why is there no hint of it in this, his longest discussion of marriage?

1 CORINTHIANS 8–10:
THE SUPREMACY OF CHRIST

Before we jump into 1 Corinthians 11, we should consider the chapters between it and chapter 7. Throughout 1 Corinthians 8–10, Paul writes about freedom in Christ. We have great freedom in Christ, but even more important, we are slaves to Christ. Our responsibility to our brothers and sisters trumps all our freedoms. Here are some key verses from each of these three chapters:

Be careful, however, that the exercise of your rights does not become a stumbling block to the weak. (8:9)

Though I am free and belong to no one, I have made myself a slave to everyone, to win as many as possible. To the Jews I became like a Jew, to win the Jews. To those under the law I became like one under the law (though I myself am not under the law), so as to win those under the law. To those not having the law I became like one not having the law (though I am not free from God's law but am under Christ's law), so as to win those not having the law. To the weak I became weak, to win the weak. I have become all things to all people so that by all possible means I might save some. I do all this for the sake of the gospel, that I may share in its blessings. (9:19–23)

So whether you eat or drink or whatever you do, do it all for the glory of God. Do not cause anyone to stumble, whether Jews, Greeks or the

church of God—even as I try to please everyone in every way. For I
am not seeking my own good but the good of many, so that they may
be saved. (10:31–33)

Above all, Christ must reign supreme in our lives. Our primary focus must be on him and to spread his gospel. We should do everything we can to support this mission. With that in mind, we will consider 1 Corinthians 11, which affirms that women may prophesy. But since that will take some time to deal with properly (in the next chapter) and since what follows elucidates Paul's intention, let's briefly skip ahead to 1 Corinthians 12, which addresses spiritual gifts for all believers, including women.

1 CORINTHIANS 12: SPIRITUAL GIFTS

Chapter 12 repeatedly asserts that God gives spiritual gifts to all believers:

Now to each one the manifestation of the Spirit is given for the common
good. To one there is given through the Spirit a message of wisdom,
to another a message of knowledge by means of the same Spirit, to
another faith by the same Spirit, to another gifts of healing by that one
Spirit, to another miraculous powers, to another prophecy, to another
distinguishing between spirits, to another speaking in different kinds
of tongues, and to still another the interpretation of tongues. All these
are the work of one and the same Spirit, and he distributes them to
each one, just as he determines. (12:7–11)

Notice that the text makes no distinction between men and women—gifts are given as the Spirit decides to distribute them. However, nobody really disputes that women are gifted. The only thing that is disputed is how women can use their gifts. And the most controversial gift is that of teaching. So we will skip down a bit to the discussion about the gift of teaching:

> *Now you are the body of Christ, and each one of you is a part of it. And God has placed in the church first of all apostles, second prophets, third teachers, then miracles, then gifts of healing, of helping, of guidance, and of different kinds of tongues. Are all apostles? Are all prophets? Are all teachers? Do all work miracles? Do all have gifts of healing? Do all speak in tongues? Do all interpret? Now eagerly desire the greater gifts.* (12:27–31)

In most passages about spiritual gifts, Paul does not specify any order of importance. However, here he does rank the following gifts in this order of importance:

1. Apostles
2. Prophets
3. Teachers
4. Miracle workers
5. Healers, helpers, guides, speakers of tongues

Additionally, Paul tells the whole church to "*eagerly desire the greater gifts.*" So, we should all aspire to be apostles, prophets, and/or teachers. But is there some sort of restriction when it comes to the use of certain gifts by women? We know that Junia was a female apostle (Rom. 16:7). As noted above, "apostle" means "one sent with a mission," so apostles were people sent out, as Paul was, to start new churches (Acts 13:3; 14:27; 15:40; Rom. 15:20). They were missionaries. One of their primary ministries was teaching. The original twelve apostles were eyewitnesses of the risen Jesus. Paul's basis for his repeated claims to be an apostle is that the risen Christ had sent him (Acts 9:6, 15; 22:10, 15, 21; 23:11; 26:16–23).

We know that there were female prophets because Anna was one (Luke 2:36–38), "*Philip the evangelist . . . had four unmarried daughters who prophesied*" (Acts 21:8–9), and the previous chapter gives instructions for "every woman who prays or prophesies" (1 Cor. 11:5). Prophets, both men and women, have special prominence throughout the Bible, and Paul repeatedly encourages all to prophesy. Prophecy in the New Testament can be defined as preaching inspired by the Holy Spirit. Teaching was an integral part of prophecy, as "so that all may learn" in 1 Cor. 14:31 makes clear.

We know that there were female teachers because Priscilla was one (Acts 18:26), as were Timothy's mother and grandmother (2 Tim. 1:5). Paul even coined a word that occurs nowhere else in Greek literature to tell female elders to be "teachers of what is excellent" (Titus 2:3; see chapter 12, "Elder Requirements and Instructions"). So blanket prohibitions of teaching by women can't be right.

Since we have examples of women in the top three categories, it makes sense that women would be found in all lesser levels of gifts as well. Paul gives no indication whatsoever that women are excluded from receiving or exercising any gift.

Five

HEAD, HAIR, AND GENDER EQUALITY WHEN PROPHESYING

1 Corinthians 11

The misunderstanding of 1 Corinthians 11 is the sole reason why Christian women all over the world wear some sort of cloth on their heads and Christian men do not. Some communities assume that this passage reinforces a universal church custom that women must wear a garment over their heads in Christian worship. But does this interpretation fit Paul's wording or cultural context? First Corinthians 8–10 has just explained Paul's desire that he (and by extension, we) should strive to be all things to all people for the sake of the gospel. How does "Whatever you do, do it all for the glory of God" (10:31) relate to rules regarding proper head covering? How do such rules advance the supremacy of Christ?

Could Paul be enforcing an existing biblical mandate? No, since nowhere in the Bible is there any comparable head-covering prohibition for men or requirement for women.

Could Paul be enforcing a social norm of the time? Corinth was a Greek city until 146 BC and then a Roman city after 46 BC.

Perhaps women in Corinth were just expected to wear head coverings? But Corinth was a big city with a very diverse population—there would not have been a single social norm. If we search for sculptures of first-century Greco-Roman women, we find many examples like these:

Portrait Bust of a Woman, AD 140–
150, The Art Institute of Chicago
Public Domain

Bust of a Young Woman,
AD 30, Glyptothek Munich
Public Domain

Marble Portrait Bust of
a Woman, AD 100–120,
Metropolitan Museum of Art
Public Domain

Marble Portrait of a Young
Woman, AD 150–175,
Metropolitan Museum of Art
Public Domain

The vast majority of sculptures of women lack head coverings. A few have head coverings, but certainly not enough to indicate any kind of a societal norm requiring head coverings. Furthermore, writers from that time period such as Ovid (43 BC–AD 17) and many current historians agree that head coverings were simply not the norm.[1] Finally, while there is no consensus that the Bible gives head-covering rules, it clearly prohibits women from having "hair braided with gold":

> Similarly, I want women to pray in appropriate clothing, to adorn themselves with modesty and self-control, not with hair braided with[2] [*kai*] gold, or [*ē*] pearls or [*ē*] expensive clothing. (1 Tim. 2:9)

> Your beauty should not come from outward adornment, such as braided hair intertwined with [*kai*] gold ornaments or [*ē*] lavish clothes. (1 Pet. 3:3)

Braided hair is common in images of Hellenistic women, but "braided hair with gold," just like "pearls" and "expensive clothes," flaunted wealth. In both passages, "braided hair with [*kai*] gold" is separated by "or" [*ē*] from "pearls" or "expensive clothing." Neither passage prohibits the common wearing of braids or wearing gold by itself, a custom that could symbolize a married woman. If all women's hair were covered with a garment in church, there would be no point in prohibiting hair intertwined with gold since it would not be visible anyway.

Christians everywhere are taught that it is what is on the inside that counts—outward appearances are never what is important (beyond basic modesty). Nowhere else in the Bible is there any mandate that corresponds to the "head-covering garment" interpretation of 1 Cor. 11:2–16. In fact, the verses just cited above seem to assume that women's hair is visible. Furthermore, surviving documentation does not support that Hellenistic culture forbade men from covering their heads or required women to cover their heads. So then, why would Paul here give strict regulations regarding head-covering garments?

The answer is that he does not. This passage is *not* about head-covering garments. No word in this chapter demands a "head covering" in the sense of a garment covering the head. And with that bit of introduction, let's dive in.

PAUL PRAISES THE CORINTHIANS (1 COR. 11:2)

> I praise you because you remember me in all things and hold fast to the traditions just as I delivered them to you. (1 Cor. 11:2)

Here, Paul praises the church in Corinth for being faithful in following the traditions he taught them. But the rest of this passage seeks to correct some disgraceful behavior in the church in Corinth not addressed in the traditions—something about what hangs down from the head. Verse 2 clarifies that the disgraceful behavior addressed in verses 4–16 was not part of the original instructions and traditions Paul had taught them. This behavior must not, therefore, have been a breach of universal church custom. Paul's praise here contrasts with his introduction to the following paragraph about Corinthian abuse of the Lord's Supper:

> *In the following directives I have no praise for you, for your meetings do more harm than good.* (11:17)

Some suggest that 11:2's praise is sarcastic, but its contrast with 11:17 indicates that 11:2's praise is sincere. Paul next states the principle behind the instructions that follow: the importance of respect for one's source.

WHAT DOES "HEAD" MEAN? (1 COR. 11:3)

But I want you to understand that the source [head] of every man is Christ, and the source [head] of woman is the man, and the source [head] of Christ is God. (11:3)

The key question that has been debated at length regarding this verse is, "What does 'head' mean in these three parallel statements?" The Greek word here is *kephalē*, which when used literally means "head" (that thing on top of your shoulders). The primary two competing explanations are "authority over" (as in "the head of a company") and "source" (as in "the head of a river").

Recently, some people have suggested "preeminence," a meaning not listed for *kephalē* in standard dictionaries, though it is related to the meaning "apex." "Preeminence" means "the quality of being more important or better than others." It is typically used to highlight the importance or significance of one particular entity over all related entities. "Preeminence" is not a natural word to compare only two entities, nor is it a natural word to use regarding entities of different classes, like these three pairs. Nothing in the context explains any of these pairs as the preeminence of the other: "The preeminence of every man is Christ, and the preeminence of the woman is man, and the preeminence of Christ is God." These three pairs are not listed in order of eminence. And preeminence is unrelated to head coverings.

Due to the significance of this issue, I now provide detailed evidence why I am so confident that "head" here does not mean "authority over" but does mean "source."

- Paul does not list the subject of each pair in hierarchal order. If "head" meant "authority," then the natural way to express the authority would either be from the top down—God is the authority over Christ, Christ is the authority over man, and man is the authority over woman—or the reverse, in ascending order of authority. But Paul's sequence does neither.
- The order given, however, does match the historical sequence of these source relations.
  - First, man came through Christ: *"Jesus Christ, through whom all things came"* (1 Cor. 8:6); 1 Cor. 11:7 refers to this event, man created in the image of God.
  - Then woman came from man, created from the man's rib, cited in 1 Cor. 11:8, 12.
  - Finally, to provide redemption, Christ came from God to become incarnate.
- The only reference in this chapter to authority is an affirmation of the woman's authority over her head in verse 10. Other than that one verse, authority is not discussed at all. But 1 Cor. 11:8 and 12 specifically discuss source relationships: "Who came from whom?"
- If "head" means "authority," then Paul would be saying that "the God" is the authority over the risen Christ. But nowhere does the Bible teach a hierarchy of authority within the eternal persons of the Trinity. Furthermore, early church councils affirm that the persons of the Trinity are equal in being, power, and glory and deny the eternal subordination of the Son to the Father.[3]

- Greek dictionaries since the twelfth century commonly assign the meaning "source" to *kephalē* ("head") but cite no pre-New-Testament examples meaning "authority."[4] The standard LSJ Greek dictionary assigns forty-nine figurative meanings for *kephalē*, including various examples meaning "source."[5] It does not, however, assign "leader," "authority," or anything similar as a meaning for *kephalē*. None of its supplements nor the lexicons by Moulton and Milligan, Preisigke, Chantraine, Woodhouse, or the twelve additional Greek lexicons cited by Cervin give even one example near Paul's time where *kephalē* means 'leader' or 'authority."[6] In spite of these facts, Wayne Grudem alleges: "All the recognized lexicons (dictionaries) for ancient Greek, or their editors, now give *kephalē* the meaning 'person in authority over' or something similar; but none give the meaning 'source.'" Much later in that book, Grudem acknowledges that the meaning "sources" "is rather standard in Greek lexicons."[7]

- "Head" clearly means "source" with no hint of authority in each of the following passages from Greek literature near the time of Paul:
  - "Of all the members of the clan here described Esau is the progenitor, the head as it were of the whole creature"[8] (Philo, *Prelim. Studies* 61).
  - "The virtuous one, whether single man or people, will be the head of the human race, [explained by the editor as 'the source of spiritual life'] and all the others like the limbs of a body which draw their life from the forces in the head and at the top"[9] (Philo, *Rewards* 125).
  - "Lust [is] the head [*kephalē* MSS A and B] of every sin" (*Apocalypse of Moses* 19.3).

- ○ "For seven spirits are established against mankind, and they are the sources [*kephalai*] of the deeds of youth"[10] (*Testament of Reuben* 2.2).

- *Rosh* means a physical head 239 times in the Hebrew Scriptures. The Septuagint (LXX) Greek version translates 226 of them *kephalē*. If *kephalē* often meant "leader" in Greek, as "head" does in English, *kephalē* would have been the obvious translation in most of the 180 instances where *rosh* means "leader." After all, the NASB translates 116 of these "head" and the ASV 115.[11] But of the 180, the best-attested text of the LXX **only once** translates *rosh* as *kephalē* that readers would have to identify as a metaphor for "leader."[12] It does this in spite of the LXX tendency to use the closest equivalent Greek word, even for meanings foreign to Greek. This shows how foreign it was for Greek to use *kephalē* as a metaphor for "leader."

- Many church fathers, including Theodore of Mopsuestia,[13] Cosmas Indicopleustes,[14] Eusebius,[15] and Photius[16] explain that each instance of "head" in 1 Cor. 11:3 means "source." For example, Cyril of Alexandria (died AD 444) writes:

  - ○ "Luke [3:28, 'Adam from God'] . . . explains the source of man, the Creator God. Thus we say that 'the head (*kephalē*) of every man is Christ,' for man was made through him and brought into existence. . . . 'And the head (*kephalē*) of woman is the man,' because she was taken out of his flesh and so indeed has him as her source. Similarly, 'the head (*kephalē*) of Christ is God,' because He is from Him according to nature: for the Word was begotten out of God the Father."[17]

Cyril of Alexandria repeatedly explains that "head" means "source":

o "Of our race he became the first head (*kephalē*), which is source (*archē*), . . . Christ . . . has been appointed head (*kephalē*), which is source (*archē*), of those who through him are being formed anew . . . he himself our source (*archē*), which is head (*kephalē*). . . . For the Word, by nature God, was begotten from Him. Because the head (*hē kephalē*) means the source (*tēn archēn*) . . . the man is said to be the head (*kephalē*) of woman, for she was taken out of him."[18]

Athanasius (circa 296–373) writes:

o For the head (*kephalē*), which is the source (*archē*) of all things, is the Son; and the head (*kephalē*), which is the source (*archē*) of Christ is God; for thus we reverently lift up all things to the One without beginning, the source (*archē*) of everything that exists through the Son.[19]

The most common objection to the view that "head" means "source" in 1 Cor. 11:3 is that the standard New Testament Greek dictionary used by most seminary students and scholars (BDAG) says that "head" denotes "superior rank," "not source."[20] Advocates of "biblical womanhood" appeal to this to assign men superior rank over women in the church and in the home. The president of Biblical Manhood and Womanhood even posted BDAG's full *kephalē* entry on his website.[21] Sadly, BDAG's *kephalē* entry contains many errors and misleading statements.

The only reason BDAG gives for denying the meaning "source" is its appeal to an article by Joseph Fitzmyer, "NTS 35, '89, 503–11." Fitzmyer's article, however, states on p. 509, "Philo uses *kephalē* in the sense of 'source,' when he speaks of Esau 'as the head of the living body, the progenitor of all the members mentioned.'" In support of the meaning "superior rank," BDAG appeals to another article by Fitzmyer, "Int 47, '93, 52–59" even though this article, pp. 53–54, cites eight additional instances in which kephalē means "source" in Greek literature. Fitzmyer, therefore, contradicted what BDAG cites him as supporting, that kephalē does not mean "source." BDAG also cites "SBedale, JTS 5, '54, 211–15," but Bedale identifies kephalē as meaning "source" and writes that "leader" was not a native Greek meaning of kephalē. The sources BDAG cites contradict BDAG's denial of the meaning "source."

To support its interpretation of "head" to mean "superior rank," BDAG changes the order of the three pairs in 1 Cor. 11:3 and also the word order within each of these pairs. It does this to make them fit a "series": "God the k[ephalē] of Christ, Christ the k[ephalē] of man, the man the k[ephalē] of the woman 1 Cor 11:3cab." It describes this series as showing "the growing distance from God . . . cp. Ps.-Aristot. De Mundo 6, 4," a passage that doesn't mention kephalē.

BDAG's "superior rank" interpretation is difficult to reconcile with Pauline Christology and conflicts with orthodox understandings of the Trinity.

BDAG adds "the" before "woman" to fit the interpretation that this refers to "the husband in relation to his wife 1 Cor 11:3b," but in this passage, there is no article or possessive before "woman" that could have signaled "wife" or any indication that this passage is only about husbands and wives.

Both Col. 2:19 and Eph. 4:15–16 use "head" to mean "source." Both use virtually identical terminology and identify "Christ" as "the head" (hē kephalē) "from whom the whole body" (ex hou pan to sōma) experiences "growth" (auxēsin). In spite of their close parallels, BDAG assigns them different meanings and does not acknowledge that either means "source."

BDAG 542 2a cites two passages in secular Greek under "in the case of living beings, to denote superior rank," but neither denotes superior rank. First, BDAG cites Artemidorus: "A man who dreamt that his father was sick got pains in his head. You already know from the first book that the head symbolizes the father."[22] This passage states nothing about "head" symbolizing "superior rank." The first book it appeals to explains instead: "The head is the source [aitios] of life and light for the whole body,"[23] and "The head resembles parents in that it is the cause [aitia] of one's living."[24] Second, BDAG states, "Zosimus of Ashkelon [500 AD] hails Demosth. as his master: ō theia kephalē." Not only is Zosimus far too late to confirm usage in Paul's day, but Demosthenes (384–322 BCE) could not have been Zosimus's master since Demosthenes had died over 800 years earlier. The standard classical Greek dictionary identifies similar salutations meaning "the noblest part."[25] The citations in BDAG give the false impression that "superior rank" was an established meaning of kephalē. BDAG's kephalē entry misrepresents various other citations as well.[26] BDAG's kephalē entry should be corrected to include the meaning "source," which fits eight of the ten occurrences of "head" in Paul's letters, the other two meaning "apex" or "top."

To summarize, ample evidence shows that "head" in 1 Cor. 11:3 means "source," not "authority over." "Source" fits the context perfectly; "authority" does not. Secular Greek dictionaries since the twelfth century commonly assign kephalē ("head") the meaning "source" but cite no pre-New-Testament examples of it that mean "authority over." The LXX Greek translation of the Hebrew Scriptures shows how foreign it was for Greek to use kephalē as a metaphor for "leader." Many church fathers explain that all three "head" references in 1 Cor. 11:3 mean "source." BDAG's entry listing the meaning "superior rank" is riddled with errors and misleading statements. I will demonstrate that the meaning "source" for *kephalē* fits Paul's argument that men and women should respect their source by not wearing hairstyles that disrespect their source.

WHAT IS DISGRACEFUL ABOUT A MAN "HAVING DOWN FROM THE HEAD"? (1 COR. 11:4)

It is time to talk about head coverings.

> Every man who prays or prophesies having [*echōn*[27]] long hair like a woman's hanging] down from his head [*kata kephalēs*[28]] disgraces his head [because this attracted illicit sexual hookups]. (11:4)

The NIV gives the impression that this refers to a head-covering garment by translating "having down from his head" as "*with his head covered.*" This, however, contradicts other commands in the Bible. Consider how Aaron was dressed in the Old Testament:

> Then bring Aaron and his sons to the entrance to the tent of meeting and wash them with water. Take the garments and dress Aaron with the tunic, the robe of the ephod, the ephod itself and the breastpiece. Fasten the ephod on him by its skillfully woven waistband. **Put the turban on his head** and attach the sacred emblem to the turban. Take the anointing oil and anoint him by pouring it on his head. Bring his sons and dress them in tunics and **fasten caps on them**. Then tie sashes on Aaron and his sons. The priesthood is theirs by a lasting ordinance.

Then you shall ordain Aaron and his sons. (Ex. 29:4–9)

Did you notice? Aaron wore a holy turban on his head, and his sons wore holy caps. Similar statements occur repeatedly, as in Leviticus:

> This is how Aaron is to enter the Most Holy Place: He must first bring a young bull for a sin offering and a ram for a burnt offering. He is to put on the sacred linen tunic, with linen undergarments next to his body; he is to tie the linen sash around him and put on the linen turban. These are sacred garments; so he must bathe himself with water before he puts them on. (Lev. 16:3–4)

In the Old Testament, priests were commanded to wear head coverings. That head covering was sacred. It symbolized piety not disgrace.

Do you see the problem this raises for thinking that Paul here prohibits men from wearing a head-covering garment? The Old Testament states clearly that priests were supposed to wear something on their heads, especially when performing religious duties. When men cover their heads in worship, therefore, they cannot be doing something that is inherently against God's will or disgraceful. Is Paul now saying the opposite, that wearing a head covering in worship is disgraceful?

Or is it that we misunderstand 1 Cor. 11:4? Interlinear Greek-English Bibles show that the phrase the NIV translates "*with his head covered*" in Greek is actually "having down from the head." So the verse actually reads, "Every man who prays or prophesies having down from the head dishonors his head." Because this sounds awkward in English, translators changed it to make it sound more natural. What is Paul talking about? What hangs "down from the head"?

This passage finally made sense to me one day while doing research at Cambridge. I found a study that cites over one hundred passages from classical antiquity, the largest number from Paul's time, that railed against men with effeminate hairstyles. In many cases, effeminate hairstyles solicited illicit sexual hookups, particularly in the Dionysiac cult near Corinth.[29] Dionysus, the god of wine, is often depicted effeminately or as partly male and partly female. Dionysiac revelries on Mount Parnassus near the Gulf of Corinth were infamous for immoral sexual practices.[30] These practices near Corinth explain why Paul prohibits Corinthian men from leading worship with long hair. Paul was clearly concerned about this because he mentions earlier in this letter those who "*will not inherit the kingdom of God*," "*the sexually immoral . . . adulterers . . . men who have sex with men . . . the greedy. . . . That is what some of you were*" (1 Cor. 6:9–11). The NIV notes "*men who have sex with men*" translates two Greek words that refer to the passive and active participants in homosexual acts. As explained below, 1 Corinthians 11 tells worship leaders not to use hairstyles that were commonly used in Corinth to attract illicit sexual liaisons.

This opened my eyes to a whole new way of understanding 1 Cor. 11:4 and 7–8. The answer that best explains what is "down from the head" is hair. The following verses contain many references to hair. Paul is talking about hair, not head-covering garments—specifically, having long hair that hangs down. It was not wrong for men to wear head coverings. In fact, it was customary for leaders in Roman worship (Corinth was a Roman city at this time) to drape a garment over their heads, the *capite velato* custom. This was not disgraceful, but a sign of piety. However, it *was* disgraceful for men to display long, effeminate hair. Paul opposed allowing men to lead worship with effeminate hair because those hairstyles were known to attract illicit sexual liaisons. First Corinthians 11:4 addresses the shame a man brings on himself and on Christ, his creator/source, when praying and prophesying with long, effeminate hair.

WHAT IS DISGRACEFUL ABOUT A WOMAN'S UNCOVERED HEAD? (1 COR. 11:5–6)

And every woman who prays or prophesies with her hair hanging down loose [like an accused adulteress, literally "head uncovered"] disgraces her head, for she is one and the same with the convicted adulteress who is shaved. For if a woman does not cover her head with her hair, she should cut her hair off. But if it is disgraceful for a woman to cut off or shave her hair, she should cover her head with her hair. (11:5–6)

Paul assumes that women are praying and prophesying in church meetings just like the men. New Testament churches were small groups that met at someone's home—teaching was not limited to a sermon from a "pastor." Men and women were participating fully in Christian worship.

Some Bibles insert "veil" and "unveiled" into their translations, including the NRSV, RSV, JB, and NEB. But veiling was an oriental custom that was uncommon in the Hellenistic world. Evidence for veiling in Hellenistic literature, pictures, and sculptures is meager indeed. Paul actually never uses the word "veil" (*kalumma*) in this passage even though he uses it four times in 2 Cor. 3:14–16. The Greek phrase *akatakalyptō tē kephalē* in 11:5 simply means "with uncovered head." It does not specify what the covering is. If Paul had wanted to convey the specific idea of a veil, he could have used the word for veil, *kalumma*, but he does not. And what does removing a veil or other head-covering garment have to do with shaving a woman's head? They have no obvious interconnection.

What would be very helpful is if we found another Bible passage about uncovering a woman's head to help us understand this passage. Numbers 5 is precisely such a passage. It concerns the situation when a man's wife is suspected of adultery, but there is no witness to the act. In this case, the woman is given the "bitter water" test to prove her guilt or innocence. An entire book of the Mishna, Tosephta, and Talmud is devoted to the "bitter water" test. So it was a prominent issue. The test begins by "uncovering" the woman's head:

> And the priest shall set the woman before the LORD, and **uncover the woman's head**, and put the offering of memorial in her hands, which is the jealousy offering: and the priest shall have in his hand the bitter water that causeth the curse. (Num. 5:18 KJV)

The Greek Old Testament (LXX) uses words similar to 1 Cor. 11:5's in Num. 5:18: *apokalypsei tēn kephalēn tēs gynaikos*, "uncover the head of the woman." However, virtually all recent Bible translations correctly reflect the Hebrew original and show that this does not mean the priest is removing something from her head. Rather, it refers to letting her hair down, as seen in the NIV:

> After the priest has had the woman stand before the Lord, he shall **loosen her hair**[31] and place in her hands the reminder-offering, the grain offering for jealousy, while he himself holds the bitter water that brings a curse. (Num. 5:18)

The only occurrence of the identical word that Paul uses in 11:5 for "uncovered" in the Greek Old Testament, in Leviticus 13:45, is also about an "uncovered head" (NASB 1977 translating *hē kephalē autou akatakalyptos*). This translates the same Hebrew word in Num. 5:18 that refers to hair let down loose. Virtually all recent Bible translations agree it means "to let their hair be unkempt"— that is, "to let the hair on the head hang down loosely."

> *HALOT* 3:970 "with רֹאשׁ ['head'] . . . Lv 10_6 13_{45} $21_{10...}$ to let down the hair of a wife accused of Infidelity . . . Nu 5_{18}."

These two passages confirm our answer: "uncovering a woman's head" refers to "loosening her hair" or "letting her hair down." Consequently, when her hair is put up on her head, her head is "covered." This understanding is further confirmed in verse 15: "Long hair is given to her as a covering."

When a woman's hair was let down loose, it symbolized undisciplined sexuality.[32] The reason Paul opposed allowing women to lead in worship with their hair let down was that this symbolized their sexual availability. In effect, when a woman did this, she accused herself of adultery. And in Paul's day, if a woman was convicted of adultery, her hair was cut off. This explains why all those pictures of sculptures I showed you earlier had women with long hair put up. This also explains why 11:5 says that a woman who uncovers her head by letting her hair down is "one and the same as the shorn woman." Paul wants such a woman to appreciate the shame she causes both to herself and to her husband by letting her hair down loose.

Paul contrasts the two alternatives in verse 6. One alternative is *"have her hair cut off."* This matches the punishment of the woman found guilty of adultery. The other alternative (and Paul's preference) is his ongoing command to cover her head. But Paul is not talking about a garment. He means she should cover her head with her long hair. If she will not do this, she should accept the shame of the punishment for adultery by cutting off her hair. As verse 15 confirms, a woman covers her head by putting her long hair up so that it covers her head.

Why would women let their hair down to prophesy in the church in Corinth? Dionysiac revelries were infamous because women (called "maenads") let their hair down, uttered ecstatic "prophecy," and engaged in orgies. Pervasive Dionysiac influence in Corinth, with its strong emphasis on freedom from cultural restraints, best explains why at least one man in the church in Corinth would display effeminate hair. Apparently as well, at least one woman in the Corinthian church, perhaps wanting to express her freedom in Christ, let her hair down when praying or prophesying. The reason Paul prohibits praying or prophesying with these Dionysiac-inspired hairstyles is probably because of their cultural association with attracting illicit sexual liaisons.

WHY A MAN OUGHT NOT COVER HIS HEAD (1 COR. 11:7–9)

For a man ought not cover his head [with long hair like women do] since he is the image and glory of God. It is the woman [not another man] who is the glory of man. For man did not come from woman, but woman from man; and neither was man created for the woman, but woman for the man. (1 Cor. 11:7–9)

These verses have been horribly misinterpreted and misapplied to women for two thousand years. They have been construed to mean that women are not created in the image of God, but rather in the image of man, and that women were created to serve men.

This passage may seem difficult to understand at first, but understood in the context I just described, it makes perfect sense. So far, Paul has told us that:

- Men should not pray or prophesy with long hair hanging down.
- Women should not pray or prophesy with long hair hanging down.
- Women should cover their heads by putting their hair up while praying or prophesying.

There is, then, one missing case: "Is it okay for a man with long hair to put his hair up, thereby covering his head?" Paul discusses that case in these verses and states, "A man should not cover his head with long hair like women do." If a man with long hair should not let it hang down, and he should not put it up, then he should not have long hair at all—and Paul makes that exact point in a few verses. But first, consider the reasons Paul gives to explain why men should not cover their heads with long hair like a woman.

The situation here is that a man has long hair and is putting it up, covering his head, like a woman would do with her long hair, thereby presenting himself as a mate for men. Regarding both male and female worship leaders, Paul prohibits behavior that in Corinth solicits illicit sexual liaisons. Such promiscuity conflicts with Christian sexual morality.

So Paul tells men not to do this because:

- **"Man . . . is the image and glory of God."** When translators use the expression "**the** image," it can give the false impression that man exclusively is *the* image and glory of God and therefore, women are not the image of God. But there is no article "the" in the Greek text. Man is not the only image bearer of God. We know from Genesis that God made both man and woman in God's image. Recall that "*God created mankind in his own image, in the image of God he created them; male and female he created them*" (Gen. 1:27).

  Paul teaches that man is created in God's image and displays the glory of God's creativity. Consequently, he should accept himself for who he is and do what brings God glory. Man should trust God's design for sexuality, which Paul immediately explains:

- **"Woman is the glory of man."** The word "glory" indicates something along the lines of pride and joy, or delight. God created woman to be man's sexual mate. Most versions translate the conjunction "but," which indicates a contrasting phrase.[33] But Paul's *de* simply indicates a continuation of his explanation. It is better translated "and" or left untranslated. It is not the Greek word that specifically means "but" (*alla*).

- **"For man did not come from woman, but woman from man; and neither was man created for the woman, but woman for the man."** Here, Paul gives two more interrelated reasons why men should not display effeminate hairstyles. God created woman from man to be man's sexual mate, and God created woman for man to be man's sexual mate, his glory, his intimate partner. Men should not display effeminate hair because it depicts a man's presenting himself as a woman, a sexual partner for other men.[34]

WHY A WOMAN OUGHT TO EXERCISE AUTHORITY OVER HER HEAD (1 COR. 11:10)

On account of this, woman ought to exercise authority over her own head, on account of the angels. (1 Cor. 11:10)

There are three parts of this verse that have often been misunderstood:

1. "on account of this"
2. "ought to exercise authority over her own head"
3. "on account of the angels"

We will consider them in order:

"**On account of this**": Every other time Paul uses the combination of "on account of this [*dia touto*] . . . on account of [*dia*] . . . ," he uses *dia touto* to apply the reasons just stated to what follows.[35] Consequently, "on account of this" should be understood as "therefore." In verses 7–9, Paul gave several reasons why male worship leaders should not style their hair like a woman does. Each is also a good reason for a woman not to loosen her hair:

- Man "*is the image and glory of God*," so his wife should not dishonor him by letting her hair down in public, because that symbolized undisciplined sexuality.
- "*Woman is the glory of man*," so she should bring glory to her husband, not shame.
- Woman was made "*from man*," so she should respect her source, not humiliate him.
- Woman was made "*for man*," to fulfill and befriend him, not to shame him.

"Ought to exercise authority over her own head": This has at times been unjustifiably altered. Many translations even drastically change this verse to make it refer to a sign of her husband's authority over her:

> For this reason, and because of the angels, the woman ought to have a sign of authority on her head. (1 Cor. 11:10 NIV 1984)

But there is nothing in this verse that even remotely justifies inserting "symbol" or "sign" or "veil" here. "Authority" throughout the New Testament refers to one's own authority—not some sign of authority held by another person. Consequently, NIV 2011 corrects this to "*a woman ought to have authority over her own head.*"

So what does this phrase mean? The first word, "*ought,*" indicates a moral imperative. We can deduce the specific meaning of "*authority*" in this verse by simply observing Paul's similar usage of the same word (highlighted in bold) earlier in 1 Corinthians:

> But the man who has settled the matter in his own mind, who is under no compulsion but **has control over** his own will, and who has made up his mind not to marry the virgin—this man also does the right thing. (1 Cor. 7:37)

That phrase, "has control over [*exousian echei*] his own will," translates the same Greek words as "to have authority [*exousian echein*]" in 11:10. Both refer to exercising control over something. So the phrase "*ought to have authority over her own head*" simply means "ought to have control of" or "exercise control over" her own head. In other words, this teaches that the woman should exercise control over her head by putting her hair up on her head in order to avoid symbolizing undisciplined sexuality.

"On account of the angels": The context here is worship, and Paul refers to angels in the context of worship elsewhere. Earlier in 1 Corinthians he wrote:

> We have been made a spectacle to the whole universe, to angels as well as to human beings. (1 Cor. 4:9)

Paul implies that angels observe the church in 1 Tim. 5:21:

> I charge you, in the sight of God and Christ Jesus and the elect angels . . .

This fits the New Testament theme that Christian worship reflects the presence of angels before the throne of God (Matt. 18:10). If the symbolism of undisciplined sexuality and the shame it causes both a woman and her husband is not sufficient reason, *"because of the angels"* (who observe worship and report directly to God) gives one more reason why women should exercise control over their heads by not letting their hair hang loose.

MAN AND WOMAN ARE NOT SEPARATE IN THE LORD (1 COR. 11:11–12)

> Nevertheless, the more important principle is that woman is not separate from man, nor is man separate from woman in the Lord. For just as woman came from man, so also man comes through woman; and all of this comes from God. (1 Cor. 11:11–12)

Because verse 10 is about woman's obligation to exercise her own authority, verse 11 begins, "Nevertheless, **woman** is not separate from man . . ." If Paul had intended verse 10 to affirm man's authority, he should have begun verse 11, "Nevertheless, **man** is not separate from woman . . . ," as some versions, like the KJV, change it to read! Verse 11 teaches, instead, that "woman is not separate from man, nor is man separate from woman in the Lord." Consequently verse 11 is incompatible with interpretations that man **is** separate from woman because man has authority over woman.

Paul begins verse 11, "Nevertheless" (*plēn*), the word he consistently uses for "breaking off a discussion and emphasizing what is important."[36] "Nevertheless" shows that although Paul has just given different instructions for men and women, the more important principle is that in Christ men and women are "not separate" from each other. "In the Lord" specifies that Paul is now talking about believers' standing in Christ and in his body, the church.

Some versions, including the NIV, translate "separate from" (*chōris*) as "*independent of*," but most Greek dictionaries do not mention people "being independent" as a meaning of this word. Anthony Thiselton notes that "is not independent of" "adds a nuance which goes beyond the adverb χωρίς [*chōris*]."[37] This word's core meaning is "separate" or "set apart." Paul affirms here that in the Lord, men and women are not set apart from each other but are equal—both have the same standing in Christ and in his body, the church. Verse 11, therefore, explains why Paul affirms "*every woman who prays or prophesies*" in verse 5.[38]

In verse 12, Paul supports his strong affirmation that "woman is not separate from man, nor is man separate from woman in the Lord." Verse 12's "woman is from the man [*ek tou andros*]" is identical to the Greek of Gen. 2:23: "She was taken from the man [*ek tou andros*]" and so clearly refers to creation. Just as woman has her source in man, every man has his source in woman. Both owe respect to the other as their source.

"The God" (*ho theos*) is the source of "all this" (*ta panta*)—namely, man and woman. "The God" cannot exclude Christ, because Paul said in verse 3 that Christ is the "head," namely "source," of man and 1 Cor. 8:6 affirms *"Jesus Christ, through whom all things came."* In this half of 1 Corinthians, Paul typically uses *ho theos* to mean "the Godhead," with broader reference than simply to "God the Father." Similarly, "the source [head] of Christ is *ho theos"* in 11:3 *refers to Christ in the incarnation coming from the Godhead.*

Paul uses *plēn* in 11:11 to highlight how important it is that women and men are not separate in the Lord. This clearly limits what Paul could have meant by several statements earlier in this passage. First, Paul must not have intended the "head" relationships in verse 3 to teach a hierarchy of man over woman. Second, he must not have intended verse 7 to imply that woman was not created in the image of God. Third, he must not have intended verse 8's statement that woman came from man to imply any subordination of woman to man.

Remember back in Genesis 2, when we discussed whether the fact that man was created before woman indicated that man held some sort of authority or special leadership role over woman? I said we would consider later what Paul says about woman coming from man. Well, here it is. Paul says that just as woman came from man, now every man is born through woman. Both owe respect to the other as their source. And all this comes from the Godhead. Paul affirms that "woman is not separate from man, and man is not separate from woman" in the context of men and women leading worship in prayer (its vertical dimension) and prophecy (its horizontal dimension). Therefore, there should be no doubt that this principle of no separation between man and woman in the Lord applies to leadership in worship.

LONG HAIR DISGRACED MEN BUT, AS A COVERING, WAS WOMEN'S GLORY (1 COR. 11:13–16)

Judge for yourselves: Is it proper for a woman to pray to God with her hair let down loose? Does not the very nature of things teach you that if a man has long hair, it is a dishonor to him, but that if a woman has long hair, it is her glory? For her long hair is given to her for a covering. But if anyone wants to cause contention, we, the churches of God, have no such custom. (1 Cor. 11:13–16)

Paul's concluding remarks confirm that it is a dishonor for a man to have long hair but that woman's long hair is her glory if she uses it as a covering rather than letting it loose in a display of undisciplined sexuality. Contemporary literature and art confirm both statements. Nobody should be contentious about this in church.

Several statements in these last few verses should remove any doubt that hair is the covering Paul is talking about. First, Paul would not have written "Judge for yourselves" if he were requiring women to wear a garment, because Hellenistic women are usually not depicted or described as wearing a head-covering garment, so they would almost certainly not judge this as improper.

Second, he affirms that "if a woman has long hair, it is her glory." Nothing in the immediate context indicates that hair is a glory that should be covered. Rather, Paul affirms that long hair is her natural glory. This affirmation would undermine Paul's argument if he intended that women should cover their hair with a garment.

Third, he affirms that "long hair is given to her as a covering." Here for the first and only time in this paragraph, Paul uses the word for a head-covering garment. He does it not to require one, but to assert that a woman's hair has been given to her to serve as a head covering. Therefore, when a woman's hair is put up modestly over her head, her head is covered. A woman does not need to put a garment over her head in order to "cover" it.

The NIV translation of the last clause, "*We have no other* [toi-autēn] *practice—nor* [oude] *do the churches of God*," is not accurate. The word translated "*other*" means the exact opposite and should be translated "We have no such practice," as Greek dictionaries make clear. In this case, the KJV is correct:

We have no such custom . . . (1 Cor. 11:16 KJV)

The conjunction Paul uses here, *oude*, is the one he typically uses to join two elements to convey a single idea (I will discuss *oude* more in the section on Gal. 3:28). Paul does not distinguish himself from the churches but identifies with them, as he always does elsewhere, so this is probably best translated: "We, the churches of God, have no such custom." Paul concludes that the churches of God have no custom like these novel Corinthian hairstyles that undermine Christian morality.

Many statements in the literature of Paul's day confirm that both men with long effeminate hair and women who let their hair down were widely regarded as shameful. Today, however, long hair on men is not regarded as shamefully effeminate, nor does it solicit immoral liaisons with other men. Nor is a woman's hair draped over her shoulders regarded as shameful; it no longer symbolizes undisciplined sexuality, nor is it a valid basis for divorce. If Paul were writing today, he would not prohibit either, nor should we.

Finally, as we conclude comments on this passage, I want to remind you that the reason we have considered this passage on hairstyles in detail is because for almost 2,000 years some have used it to claim that:

- Men have authority over women.
- Women need to have men in authority over them.
- Women must wear a garment on their head as a symbol of man's authority over them.
- Women were created to serve men.
- Women were not created in the image of God but in the image of man.
- Jesus is eternally subject to God the Father, even in heaven.

Each of these has been justified by misunderstandings and bad translations of this passage. These have resulted in injustices and abuses against women by men who believe that they have God-given power over women. This is the true "slippery slope" (more like a cliff) of not allowing women authority and leadership equal to men.

NOTES

1. Ovid (*Ars am.* 3:135–68) illustrates "that the different ways of dressing the hair in Rome were equal in number to the acorns of a many-branched oak, to the bees of the Hybla . . . every new day adding to the number." Juvenal (*Sat.* 6.501–503) writes how "important is the business of beautifications; so numerous are the tiers and storeys [sic] piled one upon another on her head!" It does not make sense that art depicted respectable women with elaborate hairstyles in such a profusion of variations but that those women never showed their hair in public. Cf. Cynthia L. Thompson, "Hairstyles, Head-Coverings, and St. Paul: Portraits from Roman Corinth," BA 51, no. 2 (June 1988): 101; Torsten Jantsch, "Die Frau soll Kontrolle über ihren Kopf ausüben (1Kor 11,10). Zum historischen, kulturellen und religiösen Hintergrund von 1Kor 11,2–16," 97–144 in *Frauen, Männer, Engel: Perspektiven zu 1Kor 11,2–16* (ed. Torsten Jantsch; Biblisch-Theologische Studien 152; Neukirchen-Vluyn: Neukirchener Verlag, 2015).

2. The NIV incorrectly translates *kai* "or."

3. For further discussion, see Kevin Giles, *Jesus and the Father: Modern Evangelicals Reinvent the Doctrine of the Trinity* (Grand Rapids: Zondervan, 2006).

4. The ninth century lexicographer Photius explained *kephalē* in 1 Cor. 11:3 as "procreator" (*gennētōr*) and "originator" (*proboleus*). K. Staab, ed., *Pauluskommentare aus der griechischen Kirche aus Katenenhandschriften gesammelt und herausgegeben: Fragmenta commentarii in Rom–2 Cor. Neutestamentliche Abhandlungen* 15 (Münster: Aschendorff, 1933), 544–83, at 567.1–2. "Source" is listed as a meaning of *kephalē* in the twelfth-century Johannes Zonaras *Lexicon*; the sixteenth-century lexicons by Henri Petrina, 1568, "head" = "source or origin"; Henri Estienne, 1572, 4:1499, "head" = "fountain-head, source, origin, cause"; Guillaume Budé, Jacobus Tusanus, Konrad Gesner, and Hadrianus Junius; and later lexicons by Franz Passow; J. G. Schneider; Wilhelm Pape, "head of a river, the source, Herodotus 4, 91"; Carlo Schenkl, 467, "head of a river = "source, spring"; S. C. Woodhouse, 390, "head = source, origin in prose and verse"; A. Bailly, 1085, "the source of a river"; Rudolf Bölting; Valentin Christian Friedrich Rost; Karl Feyerabend, 220, "head = source"; Franco Montanari, *The Brill Dictionary of Ancient Greek*, ed. Madeleine Goh and Chad Schroeder (Leiden/Boston: Brill, 2015), 1120, "beginning, origin Orphic Fragment 21a . . . of a river pl. sources Herodotus 4.91.2, of muscles Galen 4.565 d"; Robert Banks, *Etymological Dictionary of Greek* (Leiden/Boston: Brill, 2016), 1:682, "source." For full bibliography and original language citations, see the bibliography at www.pbpayne.com.

5. LSJ 945, *Supplement* 83.

6. E. A. Barber with assistance of P. Mass, M. Scheller, and M. L. West, *Supplement* (Oxford: Clarendon, 1968), 83; R. Renehan, *Greek Lexicographical Notes: A Critical Supplement to the Greek-English Lexicon of Liddell-Scott-Jones*, Hypomnemata 45 (Göttingen: Vandenhoeck & Ruprecht, 1975), 120; P. G. W. Glare with assistance of A. A. Thompson, *Revised Supplement* (Oxford: Clarendon, 1996), 175–76; Richard S. Cervin, "Does Κεφαλή [*Kephalē*] Mean 'Source' or 'Authority Over' in Greek Literature? A Rebuttal," *Trinity Journal* 10 NS (1989): 85–112, at 86–87 concludes similarly.

7. Grudem, *Evangelical Feminism*, 206, 590 n. 85.

8. Colson, LCL, *Philo* 4:488–89.

9. Colson, LCL, *Philo*, 8:389.

10. LSJ 945, OTP 1:782. Although Grudem refers to these passages, he has repeatedly asserted that "the alleged meaning 'source without authority' has still not been supported with *any* citation of *any* text in ancient Greek literature." Grudem's italics, *Evangelical Feminism*, 202.

11. They translated some with other words, such as "chief priest," which sounds better in English than "head priest."

12. All other alleged LXX instances were added by Origen, are explained in context to mean something other than "leader," or state *eis kephalēn*, indicating "as head" (cf. Acts 7:21) rather than as a metaphor "is head." For people unfamiliar with "head" as a metaphor for "leader," "as head" was far less jarring. This explains why the best-attested LXX text translates only 1 of these 180 places *kephalē* without an *eis* clearly a metaphor for "leader." *In sharp contrast*, in 8 of the 19 places where the Hebrew Scriptures have "head" with a lamed prefix meaning "as leader" at least one LXX manuscript translates this *eis kephalēn* ("as head"). The eight are Deut. 28:13 (which explains it to mean "above"); Judg. 10:18 (A); 11:8 (A), 9 (A), 11; 2 Sam. 22:44; Ps. 18:44; Lam. 1:5. Clearly, LXX translators regarded *eis kephalēn* ("as head") to be more appropriate for Greek readers than *kephalē* by itself. Even sophisticated readers who might from the context guess that *eis kephalēn* referred to a position of leadership probably found this less jarring than *kephalē* used by itself as a metaphor for "leader." Cf. Philip B. Payne, "What About Headship? From Hierarchy to Equality" in *Mutual by Design: A Better Model of Christian Marriage*, ed. Elizabeth Beyer (Minneapolis: CBE International, 2017), 141–160, 226–232, at 229–231.

13. K. Staab, *Pauluskommentare*, 567.1–2; PG 66.888C.

14. Cosmas Indicopleustes (6th century), *Topographia Christiana* 5.209 (PG 88:224A).

15. Eusebius, *Eccl. Theol.* 1.11.2–3.

16. Cited in Catherine Clark Kroeger, "The Classical Concept of *Head* as 'Source,'" in Gretchen Gaebelein Hull, *Equal to Serve: Women and Men in the Church and Home* Appendix III (Old Tappan, NJ: Revell, 1987), 267–83, at 278–79.

17. Cyril of Alexandria, *de recta fide ad Arcadiam et Marinam* 1.1.5.5(2).63, ACO 1.1.5, p. 76 beginning at line 20; J. Aubert, *Cyrilli Opera* (Paris: Magna Navis, 1638), 5^2.63E, my translation.

18. Cyril of Alexandria, *de recta fide ad Pulcheriam et Eudociam* 5^2.131D, ACO 1.1.5, p. 28 beginning at line 17; Aubert, *Cyrilli* 5^2.131D, my translation.

19. Quoting the Arian *Symb. Sirm.* 1 anath. 26 (PG 26:740B).

20. Bauer, Danker, Arndt and Gingrich, A Greek-English Lexicon of the New Testament and Other Early Christian Literature, 3rd ed. (Chicago/London: University of Chicago Press, 2000), 542. 2(a) includes under 'to denote superior rank': 1 Cor. 11:3abc; Eph. 1:22; 4:15; 5:23ab; and Col. 2:10.

21. http://www.dennyburk.com/wp-content/uploads/2016/09/BDAG-Kephale.pdf.

22. Robert J. White, *The Interpretation of Dreams* (Park Ridge, NJ: Noyes, 1975), 197. Roger A. Pack, *Artemidori Daldiani Onirocriticon Libri V* (Leipzig: Teubner, 1963), 260.

23. *Onir.* 1.2, White, *Dreams*, 16; Pack, *Onirocriticon*, 7.

24. *Onir.* 1.35, White, *Dreams*, 34; Pack, *Onirocriticon*, 43.

25. LSJ 945 *kephalē* 2 identifies similar salutations in Homer's *Iliad* and Julian Imperator's *Orationes*.

26. BDAG 542 *kephalē* 1(b) changes the Greek word order, giving the false impression that Galba is called "head." Cervin, "Rebuttal," 105 notes that Plutarch "is not calling Galba 'the head.'" P. W. G. Glare writes that Plutarch uses, "*kephalē* . . . in a literal sense." Cited from Wayne Grudem, "The Meaning of κεφαλή [*kephalē*] ('Head'): An Evaluation of New Evidence, Real and Alleged," in *Evangelical Feminism* Appendix 4, 552–99, at 587–88. BDAG 542, "2. a being of high status, head, fig." cites three more passages, but none of them clearly mean "a being of high status."

27. Similarly, Josephus *Ant.* VII.267 describes Memphibosthos as "having [*echōn*] hair long and unkempt."

28. Similarly, LXX Esther 6:12 describes Haman mourning *kata kephalēs*, with his Persian-styled hair untied and hanging down loose. These are not the words for covering the head with a garment used in LXX 2 Sam. 15:30 and Jer. 14:4, *epikaluptein tēn kephalēn.* Cf. David Stuttard, *Nemesis: Alcibiades and the Fall of Athens* (Cambridge, MA: Harvard University Press, 2018), 195; Andrew Bartlett, *Men and Women in Christ: Fresh Light from the Biblical Texts* (London: Inter-Varsity, 2019), 137.

29. H. Herter, "Effeminatus," *Reallexikon für Antike und Christentum* (1957) 2:620–50; cf. Philip B. Payne, "Wild Hair and Gender Equality in 1 Corinthians 11:2–16," *Priscilla Papers* 20:3 (Summer 2006): 9–18; Philip B. Payne, *Man and Woman, One in Christ: An Exegetical and Theological Study of Paul's Letters* (Grand Rapids: Zondervan, 2009), 143.

30. Livy 11:255; Pausanius 10.6.2.

31. NRSV "dishevel the woman's hair," RSV "unbind the hair of the woman's head," ESV "unbind the hair of the woman's head," NASB "let down *the hair of* the woman's head."

32. C. R. Hallpike, "Social Hair," *Man* NS 4 (1969): 256–64.

33. They treat it as though this were a *men* . . . *de* . . . ("on the one hand . . . on the other hand . . .") construction, where the Greek correlative conjunction *men* introduces one thing and *de* introduces something that contrasts with it. They mistakenly interpret the contrast as between man, who "is the image and glory of God" and woman, who "is the glory of man." In this verse, the conjunction *men* does not introduce "man is the image and glory of God." It introduces, "A man ought not cover his head." The clause that contrasts with this is not 11:7c, but 11:10 about what the woman "*ought to*" do—namely, to cover her head by putting her hair up.

34. For further discussion, see Payne, "Wild Hair," 9–18.

35. The other two "*dia touto* . . . *dia*" are 1 Thess. 3:6–7 and 2 Tim. 2:8–10.

36. BDAG 826 1c.

37. Anthony C. Thiselton, *The First Epistle to the Corinthians* NIGTC (Grand Rapids: Eerdmans, 2000), 841.

38. See Payne, *Man and Woman, One in Christ*, 190–95.

Six

DID PAUL TEACH, "WOMEN MUST BE SILENT IN THE CHURCHES"?

1 Corinthians 14:34–35

This is the most direct and clearly worded restriction on women in the whole Bible. Three times it prohibits women from speaking in church, each with no qualification. Yet many scholars try to restrict these prohibitions to a limited kind of speech. I must admit that for many years I tried valiantly to defend other interpretations of this passage, only to realize that, one after another, I was interpreting the passage in a way that no one in the early church did and in a way contrary to the obvious meaning of its words. I thought I finally had a viable interpretation by treating 14:33b, "as in all the churches of the saints" not as the end of Paul's argument in 14:33a, but, instead, as a qualifying introduction to verse 34. Perhaps, I thought, Paul was only demanding women be silent "as in all the churches of the saints"—namely, in accordance with the specific rule or rules for the silence of women that were the universal practice of the churches. This interpretation was appealing precisely because we do not know what those rules were, so we can't impose them today. But I found that no manuscript clearly supports this association of 33b with 34, and virtually the entire manuscript tradition treats 33b as a continuation of the sentence in 33a. Furthermore, I found that I was apparently the first person who had ever argued for this interpretation. Only then did I seriously consider the question of whether or not 14:34–35 was in Paul's original letter. Here we go . . .

> Women must be silent in the churches. They are not permitted to speak, but must be in subjection, as even the law says. If they desire to learn, they must ask their own husbands at home; for it is disgraceful for a woman to speak in the church. (1 Cor. 14:34–35)

This passage is as simple as it is controversial. Yes, it commands women in the churches not to speak, but to be silent. The passage repeats this command with three different wordings, each clear, simple, and with no qualification. These verses have puzzled virtually everyone who has studied them, including early church theologians, for many reasons, including these four:

First, the plain meaning of these verses contradicts many statements throughout 1 Corinthians that "all" may teach and prophesy, including verses shortly before and after 14:34–35:

> But **every woman who prays or prophesies** with her head uncovered dishonors her head. (11:5)

> I would like **every one of you** to . . . prophesy. (14:5)

> But if an unbeliever or an inquirer comes in while **everyone** is proph-
> esying, they are convicted of sin and are brought under judgment
> by all. (14:24)

> What then shall we say, brothers and sisters? When you come
> together, **each of you** has a hymn, or a word of instruction, a revela-
> tion, a tongue or an interpretation. (14:26)

> For **you can all prophesy** in turn so that everyone may be instructed
> and encouraged. (14:31)

> Therefore, my brothers and sisters, be eager to prophesy, and do not
> forbid speaking in tongues. (14:39)

It also contradicts all the Bible's affirmations that women
may speak in church, such as Col. 3:16's command to all believers,
"Teach and admonish one another with all wisdom . . .".

Second, it not only commands women's silence, it commands their subjection, "as the law says." Yet no Old Testament
law commands women not to speak or commands their subjection. Furthermore, it does not fit Paul's style or use of the
Old Testament. He almost always uses "it is written"[1] to refer
to specific Scriptures. The only two times he uses "as the law
says," Paul quotes that law: "*You shall not covet*" (Rom. 7:7) and "*It
is written in the Law of Moses*" (1 Cor. 9:8–10). Nor does Paul use the
Old Testament anywhere else to establish a rule for Christian
worship. To the contrary, he repeatedly repudiates attempts to
impose Old Testament religious regulations on believers and
affirms that believers are free from the law.[2]

Third, every other command in this letter **addresses the
church in Corinth**. But each of these commands **addresses**

"**women in the churches**." Following "all the churches of the saints," these commands clearly address women in **all** the churches. This fits a comment added later but is glaringly out of place in Paul's letter specifically to Corinth.

Finally, verses 34–35 disrupt Paul's conclusion to his argument regarding order in worship. Without 34–35, verse 33 leads naturally into verse 36, because 33 contrasts the peaceful worship in all the other churches to the disorderly worship customs the Corinthians originated:

> For God is not a God of disorder but of peace—as in all the congregations of the Lord's people . . . Or did the word of God originate with you? Or are you the only people it has reached? (1 Cor. 14:33, 36)

So how should we understand this passage? Most churches pretty much ignore it. Other churches come up with highly creative resolutions—not supported anywhere in the Bible—to allow participation by women in worship. For example, the Bible nowhere states that women can speak in church only if they are not too close to the pulpit. Other popular resolutions include limiting 14:34–35's demand for silence only to disruptive chatter or only to judging prophecies. But these resolutions should be rejected because they **permit** speech in church that 14:35 **prohibits**, namely asking questions out of a desire to learn. No, this passage does not even allow married (hence more mature) women to ask questions out of a desire to learn—it is as brutally clear as it seems.

Some scholars have argued recently that 1 Cor. 14:34–35 expresses the view of a group in Corinth who opposed Paul and that 14:36–38 refutes that view.[3] Although this is psychologically more plausible than the view that verses 34–35 express Paul's commands, none of the church fathers give any indication that 34–35 is a quotation. Nor are verses 34–35 introduced as a false prophecy. Nor are any of the other Corinthian quotations Paul refutes nearly this long. Nor do verses 36–38 refute anything that verses 34–35 state. Finally, as I will show you soon, many Greek manuscripts actually place verses 14:34–35 at the end of chapter 14, after verse 40. Scribes would not have done that if they thought that verses 36–38 refute verses 34–35. Nor would verses 36–38 refute text that begins after verse 40.

Crucial evidence shows that the best explanation of the different locations of these verses is that they were not part of Paul's original letter but were added later. Greek laws required women to be silent in public meetings. Consequently, it is hardly surprising that a typical reader who believed that women should be silent in public meetings would want to comment on Paul's calling *"all"* to prophesy throughout this chapter. It would be natural for such a reader sometime before AD 200 to add in the margin the "conventional wisdom" expressed in 14:34–35.

All Bible scholars know that various blocks of text have been added to New Testament manuscripts. You have probably seen notes in your Bible, such as the NIV at Matt. 18:11, "Some manuscripts include here the words of Luke 19:10" and at John 7:53, "The earliest manuscripts . . . do not have John 7:53–8:11." As I will soon show you, the oldest Bible in Greek marks both of these passages and also 1 Cor. 14:34–35 as later additions. Greek Orthodox scholar David Bentley Hart rejects 1 Cor. 14:34–35 as "almost certainly spurious."[4] *BasisBibel* notes that 14:34–35 contradicts 11:2–16 and is probably a later insertion.[5] The famous Roman Catholic scholar, Joseph Fitzmyer, notes that "the majority of commentators today" conclude that 14:34–35 is a later addition.[6] Textual scholar Kim Haines-Eitzen states this of "nearly all scholars now."[7] Gordon Fee, the most famous evangelical textual scholar, concluded that these verses were not in Paul's letter but were added in the margin of a manuscript and inserted by later copyists either after verse 33 or verse 40.[8]

If you're concerned that I am playing fast and loose with Scripture, I don't blame you. And I don't take it lightly. But crucial evidence shows that verses 34–35 were added at a later date. Allow me to explain further. This section will delve into the art and science of determining the original text of the Bible,[9] but I will try to keep it as simple as possible. The Bible as we know it does not come from a single manuscript that was preserved throughout history. Scholars determine its original text by comparing thousands of ancient manuscripts.

THE TWO LOCATIONS OF 1 COR. 14:34–35

One strong evidence that these two verses were not in the original text is the fact that they appear in two different locations in early manuscripts. In most manuscripts, this passage follows verse 33. However, in every surviving copy of one important group of old manuscripts, this passage comes at the end of 1 Corinthians 14, right after verse 40. We are not just talking about a few insignificant manuscripts, but this entire textual group.[10] It includes:

- Greek manuscripts D, E (= 0319, a ninth-century copy of D), F, G, 93. Capital alphabetic letters signify the most important old all-uppercase "uncial" manuscripts that were not written on papyrus (𝔓). Numbers not beginning with 0 signify later lowercase "minuscule" manuscripts.[11]
- Old Latin manuscripts ar b d e f g
- Ambrosiaster (AD 366–384), Sedulius Scottus (ninth century)

- The eighth-century Vulgate manuscript R (Reginensis in the Vatican) from a different textual group
- The original text of Greek manuscript 88, also from a different textual group, has features indicating that it was copied from a manuscript that lacked 14:34–35.[12]

This is the famous Codex Claromontanus D (06) from the sixth century:

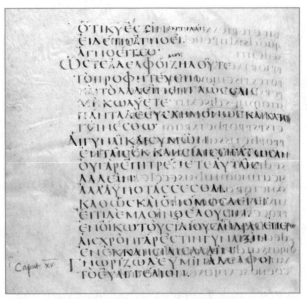

Reproduced under license from the Bibliothèque nationale de France.

In the image above, the first full paragraph beginning with an ω in the margin is 1 Cor. 14:39–40. Next is 14:34–35, beginning with ᴧ in the margin. After "Caput X̄V̄" ("chapter 15") ᴦ in the margin begins 15:1.

What could explain why 14:34–35 occurs in two different positions this far apart in different manuscripts? There are three possibilities:

1. It was originally after verse 33, and someone moved it to follow verse 40.

2. It was originally after verse 40, and someone moved it to follow verse 33.

3. Someone wrote it in the margin, and later scribes put it in the text where they thought it fit best, either after verse 33 or after verse 40.

There is no instance in any manuscript of any of Paul's letters where a passage this long was moved to a location this far away without an obvious reason. This makes possibilities (1) and (2) unprecedented, and, consequently, highly unlikely.

But scribes often inserted words into the main text that they found in the margin.

> Readers . . . react[ed] to what they read by adding comments in the margin. . . . Some of these notes could have been copied into the text by scribes who had to copy such an 'embellished' [manuscript]. . . . The inclination of scribes, at least in the view of the ancients, seems to have been toward the inclusion of marginal material into the main text.[13]

This gives strong support for possibility (3). The fourth-century Codex Vaticanus exemplifies this convention. It contains twenty instances of small readable text in the margins of the book of Matthew. All but three of them are found in the main text of virtually every subsequent surviving manuscript.

Only one explanation of why 34–35 occurs in two different places fits known scribal convention: 14:34–35 was not part of the original text but was first written in the margin of a manuscript. One or more scribes when copying this text inserted the marginal text after verse 33. This explains its usual position. Another scribe (or scribes) inserted it after verse 40. These are the only two reasonable insertion points in this vicinity. Because this is a unique case with no close parallel in any manuscript of Paul's letters, it does not undermine the authenticity of any other passage.

VATICANUS MARKS 1 COR. 14:34–35 AS A LATER ADDITION

Another evidence that verses 34–35 are a later addition is that the fourth-century Codex Vaticanus, henceforth simply called "Vaticanus," marks them as a later addition.[14] Vaticanus is one of the oldest and most important surviving manuscripts of the Greek Bible. It is the earliest manuscript that includes most of the Bible (Old and New Testaments). It has been stored at the Vatican (hence its name) since the fifteenth century. Wikipedia correctly states that "most current scholars consider Vaticanus to be one of the best Greek texts of the New Testament."[15] The Vaticanus New Testament and also its Old Testament prophetic books were penned by a single scribe, identified as "scribe B."

Before we look at these verses in 1 Corinthians 14, let me illustrate from a different verse, Matt. 18:11, how scribe B marked precisely where text was inserted. I encourage you to look this verse up in your Bible. It reads:

> **10** *See that you do not despise one of these little ones. For I tell you that their angels in heaven always see the face of my Father in heaven.* **12** *What do you think? If a man owns a hundred sheep, and one of them wanders away, will he not leave the ninety-nine on the hills and go to look for the one that wandered off?* (Matt. 18:10–12)

Notice something missing? Right; there is no Matt. 18:11. Is 18:11 in your Bible? Depending on your translation, it might have a special footnote, or be printed in italics or in square brackets. Most recent Bible versions do not include Matt. 18:11 because it is not in the earliest manuscripts and does not fit the natural flow of the text here. The vast majority of scholars have concluded that it was not part of the original text of Matthew but was inserted from Luke 19:10, where it flows naturally following the salvation of the tax collector Zacchaeus: "*For the Son of Man came to seek and to save the lost.*"

Now, consider this passage in Vaticanus. I inserted the triangle to show where Matt. 18:11 was added later. Verse 11 is not in Vaticanus:

ΤΟΥ ΕΝ ΟΥΡΑΝΟΙϹ ΤΙ Υ
ΜΙΝ ΔΟΚΕΙ ΕΑΝ ΓΕΝΗΤΑΙ

Four features in Vaticanus together specify that verse 11 was not in Matthew's original text:

1. Two dots (called a "distigme," plural distigmai) in the left margin mark the location where other manuscripts have a different text (called a "textual variant"). There are almost 800 distigmai in Vaticanus.[16]
2. A horizontal bar (called an "obelos," plural "obeloi") marks where text was added. It extends farther into the margin and is longer than most undisputed distigme-line bars marking a paragraph break.
3. The obelos is located below and to the right of the distigme.
4. A gap in the text on that same line (highlighted by my triangle) marks the precise location where a later insertion interrupted Matthew's text.

The only added text at this gap with any manuscript evidence is verse 11.

We know that scribe B made these marks because (1) only scribe B could leave a gap in the original text (later scribes could not move text that was already there), and (2) parts of some of these marks were not reinked with the rest of the manuscript, so they still display Vaticanus's original apricot-color ink. Scribe B penned fifteen distigme-obelos symbols in the New Testament. Appendix 1 provides their images. All fifteen have a gap in the marked line of text at the exact location the original text was interrupted by a widely acknowledged insertion of four or more consecutive words.

Furthermore, we know that scribe B intended horizontal bars to mark locations where text was added because scribe B actually explained three times in Isaiah that horizontal-bar obeloi mark where Vaticanus's Greek text adds words that are not in the Hebrew Scriptures.[17] Here is the one at Isa. 51:23:

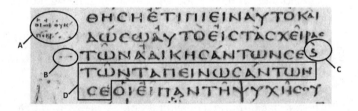

A Note the small letters in the left margin: οιωβ'ογκ'π'εβγ'. This is scribe B's abbreviation for οἱ ὠβελίσμενοι οὐ κεῖται παρ' ἑβραίοις. It means, "The [text] marked with an obelos does not occur in [the] Hebrew [text]."

B Below and to the right of that abbreviated explanation A you can see a horizontal bar obelos.

C There is a gap at the right end of that line where a later scribe added a symbol meaning "and" and shaped like an "s" with ` over it in darker ink above the baseline.

D The gap marks the precise location where the LXX Greek translation interrupted the original text by adding words not found in the Hebrew: ⲦⲰⲚ ⲦⲀⲠⲈⲒⲚⲰⲤⲀⲚ ⲦⲰⲚ ⲤⲈ ("them that humbled you," which D identifies). The added words fill the next line and begin the following line. Neither of these two lines has an obelos.

Each of Isaiah's three abbreviated obelos explanations shares key elements with all four features that mark Matt. 18:11 as added text:[18]

1. Their ⲟⲓⲱⲃ'ⲟⲩⲕ'ⲡ'ⲉⲃϥ' correspond to Matt. 18:11's distigme because both are abbreviated explanations of the location of a textual variant.
2. Both Isaiah's and Matthew's abbreviated explanations are next to a horizontal-bar obelos.
3. The horizontal-bar obelos is below and to the right of both abbreviated explanations.
4. A gap in that line of text marks the precise point where the original text was interrupted.

With that background, consider 1 Cor. 14:34–35 in Vaticanus (I added the triangle):

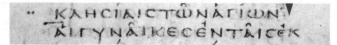

As you can see, the four previously mentioned features are also present here:

1. A two-dot distigme (an abbreviated explanation of the location of a textual variant).

2. The distigme is next to a horizontal-bar obelos.

3. The horizontal-bar obelos is below and to the right of the distigme.

4. A gap in that line of text marks the precise point where the original text was interrupted. The interruption here, too, is a widely-recognized block of added text, 1 Cor. 14:34–35.

The combination of these four features specifies that the gap marks where the original text was interrupted. The only added text with any manuscript evidence that begins at this gap is 14:34–35. As in Isa. 51:23, the gap at the end of 1 Cor. 14:33 separates the original text from the distigme-obelos-marked added text (14:34–35) on the following lines, which in both passages have no additional obeloi. Like the insertion symbol $^\top$ in the standard Greek New Testament (NA[28]), each gap in a distigme-obelos-marked line of text marks the exact point where the original text was interrupted. Whenever a gap occurs at the end of such lines of text, the interrupting text begins on the next line, or would begin on the next line if it were in the text.[19]

Why should we trust scribe B's evident judgment that 1 Cor. 14:34–35 was not in Paul's original letter? Both standard critical editions of the Greek New Testament and virtually all recent Bible translations agree with scribe B's judgment that every other block of text marked with a distigme-obelos was not in the original text of Scripture. None of these Bible versions' texts includes any of the other distigme-obelos-marked additions. Since scholarship has confirmed that scribe B was correct in every other case, 1 Cor. 14:34–35 should also be considered a later addition, especially because scribe B had access to far more pre-Vaticanus text than we have today. We know this from the wide variety of manuscripts that include the added text marked by distigme-obelos symbols and original-ink distigmai.

All this evidence supports the widely-held view that 1 Cor. 14:34–35 was not in Paul's original letter and should not be considered part of the Bible. Furthermore, 14:34–35 shares several characteristics with John 7:53–8:11, which is almost universally acknowledged as not original to the Gospel of John. Both passages occur at different locations in different manuscripts, display a high concentration of textual variations, contain word usage atypical of the book's author, disrupt the flow of the passage, and are marked as later additions by a Vaticanus distigme-obelos symbol.

Greek texts and Bibles marking John 7:53–8:11 as a later addition: NA[28], UBS[5], The Greek New Testament Produced at Tyndale House Cambridge, NIV, NRSV, ESV, CEB, CSB, NASB, JB, NEB, REB.

These distigme-obelos symbols combined with other Vaticanus evidence provide crucial new support for the *reliability* of the transmission of the text of the New Testament, including evidence that Vaticanus preserves a second-century text of all four Gospels. The key facts are:

The Vaticanus Gospels have virtually no periods at the end of sentences, even though there is a period at the end of every sentence in every Vaticanus epistle. It is highly unlikely that scribe B removed periods from the Vaticanus Gospels' exemplar for several reasons. First, periods help readers understand the text, so it is unlikely that any scribe copying a manuscript with periods would remove them. Second, since scribe B retained the periods in all the epistles, it is unlikely scribe B would change convention in the same manuscript by removing periods so consistently from the Gospels. Third, removing periods would have been contrary to all the evidence that scribe B took extraordinary care to preserve the original text, punctuation, and symbols in the margins of the manuscripts scribe B copied to create Vaticanus.[20]

All this shows that Vaticanus's Gospels preserve an early text unaffected by the addition of periods. Vaticanus's epistles, however, preserve a later text that was written after periods had been added. It is because the Vaticanus epistles' text is later that the one distigme-obelos-marked addition in the epistles, 1 Cor. 14:34–35, is in the Vaticanus text. Scribe B faithfully preserved the source manuscript's addition of 14:34–35 but marked it as spurious just as scribe B also preserved the additions throughout the Vaticanus prophetic books but used obeloi to signify that none of them were in the Hebrew text.

Several lines of evidence show that the text of the Vaticanus Gospels is even earlier than the text of papyrus 75 (henceforth $\mathfrak{P}^{75}$), which contains most of Luke and John. Bruce Metzger dated $\mathfrak{P}^{75}$ to AD 175–225.[21] First, unlike the Vaticanus Gospels, $\mathfrak{P}^{75}$ has periods after every sentence. Even the older $\mathfrak{P}^4$ has many periods. Second, the Vaticanus Gospels' text has only half as many abbreviated forms of holy names (nomina sacra) as $\mathfrak{P}^{75}$. The number of these abbreviated forms expanded over time. Third, some of Vaticanus's spellings are earlier than $\mathfrak{P}^{75}$'s spellings. Fourth, where differences occur on distigme-obelos lines, both standard critical editions of the Greek New Testament (NA[28], UBS[5]) judge that the text of Vaticanus is earlier than $\mathfrak{P}^{75}$'s text.

Fifth, and especially important, the Vaticanus Gospels' text is so old that it contains none of the thirteen insertions its distigme-obelos symbols mark. We are confident that scribe B did not remove these additions because scribe B didn't remove:

- obelos-marked added text from their 121 occurrences in its prophetic books,
- the one distigme-obelos-marked addition in the epistles, 1 Cor. 14:34–35,
- any of the sentence-ending periods in any Vaticanus epistle,
- or even paragraph bars in Zechariah that conflict with scribe B's paragraph-break judgments.

In copying manuscripts, scribe B took great care not to change their content. Scribe B did not correct old spellings that had gone out of use or add periods at the end of sentences in the four Gospels. In twelve places scribe B wrote the abbreviation ογκ'π'εβρ' [meaning "not in Hebrew"] in the margin where Vaticanus has no obelos.[22] This shows that scribe B recognized that these words in the manuscript Vaticanus copied were not in the Hebrew but did not mark them with an obelos. It would have been much simpler just to add an obelos. But scribe B did not add an obelos because obeloi were an essential part of copies of Origen's edited LXX. To have added obeloi would cause Vaticanus no longer to faithfully reproduce the text of its source manuscript. This shows how faithfully scribe B preserved the text of Vaticanus's source manuscripts. In the New Testament, however, scribe B could add obeloi without changing anything essential to the text. Scribe B's use of obeloi shows that scribe B was well trained to preserve the source manuscripts' content.

All this supports the conclusion that, except for any errors scribe B made in copying them, the entire text of all four Vaticanus Gospels, although written in the fourth century, preserves a second-century text.

Furthermore, other manuscripts preserve all sixteen distigme-obelos-marked insertions.[23] Their 100 percent survival provides evidence that the text of most early New Testament insertions has survived. They survived even though only a small portion of the early manuscript evidence supports most of them. In sharp contrast, the first publicly distributed text of each New Testament book was the direct source of the earliest manuscripts and the ultimate source of all later copies. Consequently, we should have even greater confidence that the vast majority of the text of the first publicly distributed New Testament books has also survived.

Additionally, because textual variants have survived at over 92 percent of the locations marked by the fifty-one original-ink-color Vaticanus distigmai, these provide a separate statistical basis for confidence that early New Testament textual variants have survived remarkably well.[24]

Finally, since all distigme-obelos-marked textual judgments in all four Gospels and Acts agree with the judgments of both standard Greek New Testament texts, they confirm the reliability of the standard principles of textual criticism used to produce the New Testament in our Bibles.

1 CORINTHIANS 14:34–35: ANSWERS TO OBJECTIONS

"Those horizontal bars aren't obeloi. They're just bars that mark paragraph breaks."

Vaticanus's New Testament paragraph bars differ from distigme-obelos symbols in date, form, and function. The New Testament horizontal bars that signal paragraph breaks display clear signs of not being original. Fifty-one distigmai match the apricot color of original Vaticanus ink, and four distigme-obelos symbols contain original-apricot-color ink. In contrast, none of

Vaticanus's New Testament paragraph bars match its original ink color, even though Vaticanus has over three times more paragraph bars than distigmai.[25] Clearly, therefore, scribe B did not pen these paragraph bars. Many scholars agree that these paragraph bars are later additions. Originally, therefore, scribe B's distigme-obelos symbols could not have been confused with surrounding paragraph bars. Furthermore, only the original scribe could insert the distigme-obelos-line gaps.

All of scribe B's obeloi in distigme-obelos symbols share five characteristic features: they (1) underscore a distigme-marked line, (2) extend farther into the margin and (3) are longer than most undisputed distigme-line paragraph bars, (4) occur by lines where some manuscripts contain additions of four or more consecutive words, and (5) have a gap precisely where manuscripts listed by NA[28] and/or Reuben Swanson insert four or more consecutive words.[26]

In sharp contrast, all thirty-one paragraph bars that randomly occur by a line with a distigme lack at least two of these five characteristic features. As appendix 2 illustrates, even just the combination of the distigme-line obelos bars' extension into the margin and length sets them apart from all except one (1395C) of the thirty-one distigme-line undisputed paragraph bars.

If someone had intended these sixteen bars with these five characteristic features to be merely paragraph bars, as this objection assumes, it is virtually impossible that they would **all** coincide with four-or-more-consecutive-word interruptions of the prior text because interruptions of four or more consecutive words occur on average only once in 83.5 lines of Vaticanus text.[27]

However, since distigmai mark places where variants occur, variants—including insertions—are far more likely to occur in distigme lines than in random lines of Vaticanus. This explains why three of the thirty-one distigme lines that randomly occur with a paragraph bar coincide with an interruption of four or more consecutive words. The standard chi-square test calculates that if bars with these characteristics were paragraph bars unrelated to multi-word insertions, the probability of such sharply contrasting proportions occurring is less than 1.5 in 100 million.[28]

Furthermore, if the obelos in every distigme-obelos symbol were merely a paragraph bar, as this objection contends, why do all fifteen interruptions that the original distigme-obelos symbols mark occur precisely at the gap in those lines? The only natural explanation of the precise positioning of each of these multiword interruptions at a gap is that the original scribe B, who alone could insert gaps, marked these insertion points with gaps and added distigme-obelos symbols to indicate this.

"All manuscripts that include text from this part of 1 Corinthians include 1 Corinthians 14:34–35, so it must be original text."

This objection ignores the fact that a single manuscript can record differing readings and that different readings in the same manuscript are assigned separate manuscript symbols because they preserve different texts. Codex Fuldensis, one of the oldest Latin manuscripts (AD 546–547), includes 14:34–35 after 14:33, but the early manuscript expert, Bishop Victor of Capua, who commissioned Fuldensis, had his original scribe write replacement text in the bottom margin that omits 14:34–35.[29] Bishop Victor's corrected text has its own manuscript symbol, and that text does not include 14:34–35. Vaticanus's distigme-obelos-corrected text (symbol B¨–) doesn't include 14:34–35 either. Its distigme-obelos identifies an original text without 14:34–35. Furthermore, Greek manuscript 88's original text doesn't include 14:34–35 after 14:33, and Clement of Alexandria (*Paed.* 3.11), on the silence of "woman and man," appears to presuppose a text without 14:34–35.[30] These manuscripts all support the omission of 14:34–35.

"Only an extraordinarily early addition of 14:34–35 could explain its presence in every manuscript."

In fact, 1 Cor. 14:34–35 could have been introduced well into the second century and still explain all the textual data. For example, virtually all critical editions of the Greek New Testament agree that originally there was no verb "submit" in Eph. 5:22.[31] The fourth-century Codex Sinaiticus (א) is the earliest New Testament manuscript with "submit" in Eph. 5:22. Nevertheless, every surviving manuscript written after Sinaiticus that contains Eph. 5:22 includes "submit." This shows how quickly this widely acknowledged addition became part of every subsequent surviving manuscript. The addition of "submit," like 1 Cor. 14:34–35, reinforced "conventional wisdom" regarding women. This probably accelerated the adoption of both. The rapid universal adoption of "submit" shows that the addition of 14:34–35 even well into the second century could easily explain its presence somewhere in every surviving manuscript of this part of 1 Corinthians.

Manuscripts from at least the fourth century illustrate the far greater tendency to add text than to remove text. For example, Vaticanus's prophetic books have 121 obeloi marking locations where words were added that are not in the Hebrew text, but only twelve asterisks marking locations where Hebrew words were left untranslated. Furthermore, once 1 Cor. 14:34–35 was in the text, scribal convention made removing it highly unlikely.

NOTES

1. Rom. 1:17; 2:24; 3:4, 10; 4:17, 23; 8:36; 9:13, 33; 10:5, 15; 11:8, 26; 12:19; 14:11; 15:3, 4, 9, 21; 1 Cor. 1:19, 31; 2:9; 3:19; 4:6; 9:9, 10; 10:7, 11; 14:21; 15:45, 54; 2 Cor. 4:13; 8:15; 9:9; Gal. 3:10, 13; 4:22, 27.

2. Rom. 6:14–15; 7:4–6; 10:4; 1 Cor. 9:20–21; Gal. 2:19; 3:13, 23–25; 5:18; Eph. 2:15.

3. See Philip B. Payne, "Is 1 Corinthians 14:34–35 a Marginal Comment or a Quotation? A Response to Kirk MacGregor," *Priscilla Papers* 33, 2 (Spring 2019): 24–30.

4. David Bentley Hart, *The New Testament: A Translation* (New Haven/London: Yale, 2017), 345–46.

5. *BasisBibel* (Stuttgart: Deutsche Bibelgesellschaft, 2021), 1788.

6. Joseph A. Fitzmyer, *First Corinthians*, AB (New Haven: Yale, 2008), 530.

7. K. Haines-Eitzen, *The Gendered Palimpsest: Women, Writing, and Representation in Early Christianity* (Oxford: Oxford University Press, 2012), 62. Payne, *Man and Woman, One in Christ*, 226–227 identifies fifty-five studies which conclude that 1 Cor. 14:34–35 is not original.

8. Gordon D. Fee, *The First Epistle to the Corinthians*, NICNT (Grand Rapids: Eerdmans, 1987), 699–708.

9. "Original text" here refers to the text of each individual book of the New Testament as first distributed publicly, the ultimate source of all later copies of that book.

10. Fee, *Corinthians*, 699.

11. NA[28] 792–819 lists manuscript dates, locations, and contents.

12. Philip B. Payne, "Ms. 88 as Evidence for a Text without 1 Corinthians 14.34–5," *NTS* 44 (1998): 152–58; Payne, *Man and Woman, One in Christ*, 246–51.

13. Ulrich Schmid, "Conceptualizing 'Scribal' Performances: Reader's Notes," in *The Textual History of the Greek New Testament: Changing Views in Contemporary Research*, ed. Klaus Wachtel and Michael Holmes (Atlanta: SBL, 2011), 49–64, at 62, 50, 58.

14. Philip B. Payne, "Vaticanus Distigme-obelos Symbols Marking Added Text, Including 1 Corinthians 14.34–5," *NTS* 63 (2017): 604–25, downloadable free at https://www.cambridge.org/core/journals/new-testament-studies/article/vaticanus-distigmeobelos-symbols-marking-added-text-including-1-corinthians-14345/A5FC01A6E14A2A1CF1F514A9BF93C581.

15. https://en.wikipedia.org/wiki/Codex_Vaticanus.

16. Philip B. Payne and Paul Canart, "Distigmai Matching the Original Ink of *Codex Vaticanus*: Do They Mark the Location of Textual Variants?," in *Le manuscrit B de la Bible (Vaticanus graecus 1209), Introduction au fac-similé, Actes du Colloque de Genève (11 juin 2001), Contributions supplémentaire*, HTB 7, ed. Patrick Andrist

(Lausanne: Éditions du Zèbre, 2009), 199–226, downloadable free from www .pbpayne.com under Publications: Articles.

17. There is wide scholarly consensus that horizontal-bar shaped obeloi in Greek textual analysis mark the location of a specific kind of variant, spurious added text, e.g., LSJ 1196. Origen explains in his *Commentary on Matthew* 15.14 that he used obeloi "to fix" discrepancies between the Septuagint (LXX) and both the Hebrew text and its other Greek translations by changing the LXX text to "what the other editions agreed upon. And we marked with an obelos some lines because they were not present in the Hebrew version . . . [and added original words the LXX omitted] from the other editions which agree with the Hebrew Bible." Translation from Francesca Schironi, "The Ambiguity of Signs: Critical ΣΗΜΕΙΑ [*sēmeia*] from Zenodotus to Origen," in *Homer and the Bible in the Eyes of Ancient Interpreters*, ed. M. Niehoff (Leiden/Boston: Brill, 2012), 101. The Hebrew Scriptures were Origen's "text of departure" used as the standard for correction (Schironi, "Ambiguity," 102). Scribe B copied the Vaticanus Prophets from a manuscript that reproduced some of Origen's obeloi.

18. Payne, "Distigme-obelos," 619.

19. Whenever typographically possible, NA[28] positions the text-critical symbol for insertions (ᵀ) at the end of a line when that is where the original text was interrupted. This appears to be true in every case in Matthew, even when the insertion, if it had been in the text, would have begun on the next line. In NA[28], ᵀ is at the end of a line at Matt. 6:13, 16, 26; 13:39; 14:12; 15 (twice); 15:24; 17:11; 24:31; 26:8, 27, 28, 39, 60, 71. The only cases in Matthew where NA[28] positions ᵀ at the beginning of a line appear to be necessary typographically. ᵀ must accompany the rest of the Isaiah quotation inserted into Matt. 13:14 on the next line. In every other case, there does not appear to be enough room at the end of the previous line for the ᵀ: Matt. 8:25; 10:30; 19:17; 20:23; 22:14; 25:4, 17.

20. Payne, "Distigme-obelos," 609, 621–22, 624.

21. B. Metzger, "Recent Developments in the Textual Criticism of the New Testament," *Historical and Literary Studies: Pagan, Jewish, and Christian* NTTS 8 (Leiden/Grand Rapids: Brill/Eerdmans, 1968), 145–62, at 157–58, "Since B is not a lineal descendent of 𝔓⁷⁵, the common ancestor of both carries the . . . text to a period prior to AD 175–225, the date assigned to 𝔓⁷⁵."

22. The twelve cases are: 1033 B21, 37; 1034 B31*; 1035 C8; 1038 B15; 1045 C2, 38; 1046 A40*; 1054 C16*; 1066 C30*; 1073 C36*; 1074 B17*. * = original ink.

23. One (1390A, see appendix 1) has downward dipping ink from both dots and the bar. This indicates a later hand that could not add a gap to the already existing text.

24. Cf. Payne, "Distigme-obelos," 606 and n. 8.

25. Cf. Payne and Canart, "Distigmai," 203–9, 214–15.

26. Reuben J. Swanson, ed., *New Testament Greek Manuscripts: Variant Readings*

Arranged in Horizontal Lines Against Codex Vaticanus. Matthew, Mark, Luke, John (Sheffield: Sheffield Academic, 1995); *The Acts of the Apostles* (Sheffield: Sheffield Academic, 1998); *1 Corinthians* (Wheaton, IL: Tyndale House, 2003).

27. See the calculation in note 8 at https://www.pbpayne.com/wp-content/uploads/2021/07/Critique-of-Fellows-Krans-Vaticanus-Distigme-Obelos-Denials.pdf.

28. 1.467 in 100,000,000 (= 10^8). See the calculation details on pp. 3–4 at https://www.pbpayne.com/wp-content/uploads/2021/07/Critique-of-Fellows-Krans-Vaticanus-Distigme-Obelos-Denials.pdf.

29. Philip B. Payne, "Fuldensis, Sigla for Variants in Vaticanus, and 1 Corinthians 14.34–5," NTS 41 (1995): 240–62, at 240–50, photograph at 261. For other manuscript evidence against the originality of 1 Cor. 14:34–35, see Payne, *Man and Woman, One in Christ*, 227–53.

30. Payne, "Ms. 88," 152–58; Payne, *Man and Woman, One in Christ*, 250–51.

31. For more details see below, pp. 113 and n. 6.

MAN AND WOMAN,
ONE IN CHRIST

Galatians 3:28

Galatians 3:28 provides the theological reason for Paul's repudiation of Peter's withdrawal from table fellowship with gentiles in Gal. 2:11–14. Paul repeats three times a poetic expression that most scholars believe Paul quoted from an affirmation at baptism:

There is no Jew-Greek division, there is no slave-free division, there is no male-female division, for you are all one in Christ Jesus.

"You are all **one** in Christ Jesus" shows that Paul intends to deny these **divisions**. Galatians 3:28 asserts a radically new understanding of relationships in Christ—one that repudiates divisions between Jew and Greek, slave and free, and male and female in Christ.

One key to understanding this passage is Paul's usage of the Greek conjunction *oude* between Jew and Greek and between slave and free. Paul typically uses *oude* to join two elements to convey a single idea. Paul must not mean "There is no Jew or Greek in Christ" since there are Jews in Christ and there are Greeks in Christ. Instead, Paul uses these pairs to make the single point that in Christ there is no division that separates the members of these pairs. These divisions that Paul repudiates contrast with: "You are all one in Christ Jesus."

Paul also uses *oude* to join elements to convey a single idea repeatedly in Galatians 1. He then uses "but" (*alla*) to contrast that single idea to something else:

Paul, an apostle—sent not from man and not (*oude*) through men, but (*alla*) through Jesus Christ (Gal. 1:1)

The gospel I preached is not of human origin and (*oude*) I did not receive it from any man and (*oude*) I was not taught it, but (*alla*) I received it by revelation from Jesus Christ. (Gal. 1:11–12)

I did not immediately consult with flesh and blood—(*oude*) I did not go up to Jerusalem to those who were apostles before me, but (*alla*) I went away to Arabia. (Gal. 1:16–17)

In Gal. 3:28, for "*male and female*," Paul uses a different conjunction, *kai* ("and"). But he is simply continuing the list of contrasting pairs of people while using the standard conjunction that the Bible uses to describe God's creation of "*male and female*" (e.g., Gen. 1:27; 5:2; Matt. 19:4; Mark 10:6). Paul similarly substitutes *kai* for *oude* to teach an almost identical single idea in Romans 10:12, "*There is no difference between Jew and* [kai] *Gentile*."[1] Paul's substitution of *kai* for *oude* doesn't change the meaning of 3:28's final pair. It, too, conveys the single idea, "There is no male-female division . . . in Christ."

Paul clearly intends all three pairs to be viewed in the same way because he summarizes, "*You are all one in Christ Jesus.*" The statements before and after 3:28 also affirm the same status for women as for men: "*You are all children of God through faith*" (3:26) . . . "*you are Abraham's seed, and heirs according to the promise*" (3:29).

Some allege that Gal. 3:28 applies only to who can be saved and not also to life in the church. But its historical context regarding gentile table fellowship and Jewish laws makes its application to church obvious. Furthermore, all Paul's parallel passages clearly apply to this life.

Galatians 3:28 teaches that "male-female division" does not exist in Christ. Paul's point is that gender, just as race and social rank, is irrelevant to status in Christ. Just as gentiles should have the same opportunities for service in the church as Jews,[2] and slaves should have the same opportunities for service in the church as free persons, women should also have the same opportunities for service in the church as men. Exclusion of all women from church leadership or from teaching in the church is precisely the sort of division that Gal. 3:28 repudiates. To exclude women from church leadership is an even greater restriction than not eating with gentiles. The barriers that separated male and female in Hellenistic society do not exist in the new reality of being "*one in Christ.*" It contradicts the plain meaning of "there is no male-female division in the body of Christ" to say that there is a male-female division in the body of Christ, with all females excluded from teaching men and from church leadership. Since it is contrary to the gospel to withdraw from table fellowship with gentiles (Gal. 2:11–14), it is even more contrary to the gospel to exclude gentiles, slaves, or women from church leadership.

GALATIANS 3: ANSWER TO THE KEY OBJECTION

"Galatians 3:28 is actually not about divisions in the church and the family but is only talking about who can be saved."

No. No. No! Galatians 3:28's wording, context, and parallel passages show that it must refer to actual life in the church, not just to who can be saved, and not just to individuals' relationship to God. Each of these three pairs describe social standing, so to say that they have nothing to do with social standing is to deny their most obvious meaning. Galatians is largely about an actual, physical, earthly dispute between Jews and gentiles. When Peter withdrew from table fellowship with gentiles, Paul *"opposed him to his face, because he stood condemned . . . [of] hypocrisy . . . [and] not acting in line with the truth of the gospel"* (Gal. 2:11–14). After denouncing Peter's unequal treatment of Jews and gentiles, Paul defends the equal standing of Jew and gentile in Christ and expands it to include slave and free and male and female.

If this verse did not repudiate male-female division in Christ, then no one would try to limit its application to who can be saved. After all, when Paul expresses almost the exact same thought in Colossians, we all understand that he is talking about life here on earth in Christian fellowship:

> Here there is no Gentile or Jew, circumcised or uncircumcised, barbarian, Scythian, slave or free, but Christ is all, and is in all. Therefore, as God's chosen people, holy and dearly loved, clothe yourselves with compassion, kindness, humility, gentleness and patience. (Col. 3:11–12)

And when Paul mentions similar thoughts later in Galatians, we all understand that he is talking about life here on earth in Christian fellowship:

For in Christ Jesus neither circumcision nor uncircumcision has any value. The only thing that counts is faith expressing itself through love. (Gal. 5:6)

Neither circumcision nor uncircumcision means anything; what counts is the new creation. (Gal. 6:15)

And when Paul talks about breaking down barriers between the circumcised and uncircumcised in Ephesians, we all understand that he is talking about life here on earth in Christian fellowship:

For he himself is our peace, who has made the two groups one and has destroyed the barrier, the dividing wall of hostility. (Eph. 2:14)

Consequently, you are no longer foreigners and strangers, but fellow citizens with God's people and also members of his household. (Eph. 2:19)

And when Paul talks about the body of Christ in 1 Corinthians, we all understand that he is talking about life here on earth in Christian fellowship, as at 1 Cor. 12:12–13:

Just as a body, though one, has many parts, but all its many parts form one body, so it is with Christ. For we were all baptized by one Spirit so as to form one body—whether Jews or Gentiles, slave or free—and we were all given the one Spirit to drink.

But for some reason, as soon as Paul adds the relationship between male and female, some people think he cannot possibly be repudiating divisions in the church here and now; he must be talking *only* about salvation in God's sight. But this is not so, and there are many reasons for concluding that Gal. 3:28 is actually about life here on earth in Christian fellowship:

- **Absence of dispute about salvation.** As far as we know, after Peter's miraculous experiences with Cornelius and the Spirit falling on gentiles (Acts 10:1–11:18), there was no dispute whether gentiles, slaves, or women could become Christians. Consequently, there is no reason for Paul to affirm that these specific groups can be saved. The issues in Galatia were practical life issues such as circumcision, table fellowship, and whether gentiles had to follow the Law. Throughout this letter Paul repudiates divisions in the church and affirms the oneness of the body of Christ.

- **Connection of "One in Christ" to community.** When Paul affirms that we are "one in Christ," or "all one body," he refers to relationships between people in the body of Christ, the church; he is not speaking of the individuals' spiritual state before God as though that were divorced from their interpersonal relationships. In Christ, "oneness" replaces racial, social, and biological divisions. Consequently, discrimination and special treatment based on these external factors is contrary to the unity of Christ's body, the new humanity where Jews and gentiles share equal citizenship (cf. 1 Cor. 12:12–13; Eph. 2:11–22; Col. 3:10–11). Being "in Christ Jesus" in Paul's letters applies not just to reconciliation with God, but to life in the church, such as in Gal. 2:4, *"the freedom we have in Christ Jesus"* from circumcision; Gal. 5:6, what counts "in Christ Jesus . . . *is faith expressing itself through love*"; and Eph. 2:10, we are *"created in Christ Jesus to do good works."*

- **Denial of divisions in Christ.** The entire book of Galatians is a frontal attack against granting favored status or treatment to Jews over gentiles. In this context, 3:28's "There is no Jew-Greek division . . . in Christ" denies any exclusion of gentiles from any ministry or position in the church. The absence in Christ of the distinction between Jew and gentile is the reason Paul denies the need for circumcision, the central practical issue of Galatians,[3] so Gal. 3:28 must not be restricted to spiritual status.

- **Radical newness of life in Christ.** This theme permeates Galatians, e.g. 1:4; 2:20, "*I no longer live, but Christ lives in me*"; 3:2, 5, 14, "*By faith we . . . receive the promise of the Spirit*"; 4:3, 5–7, "*You are no longer a slave, but God's child . . . an heir*"; 5:19–24, "*Those who belong to Christ Jesus have crucified the flesh with its passions and desires*"; 5:25–26, "*Since we live by the Spirit, let us keep in step with the Spirit*"; 6:15, "*What counts is the new creation.*" To interpret 3:28 as if it has nothing to do with relationships or as too extreme to be taken literally is incompatible with this radical newness of life here on earth that Paul affirms.

- **Freedom from the law in Christ.** Galatians 2:4 and following describes Paul's opposition to "*false believers* [who] *had infiltrated our ranks to spy on the freedom we have in Christ Jesus and to make us slaves.*" Galatians 3:23–25 affirms, "*We were held in custody under the law, locked up. . . . Now that this faith has come, we are no longer under a guardian.*" Paul's description of Hagar and Sarah affirms that "*the Jerusalem that is above is free, and she is our mother. . . . We are not children of the slave woman, but of the free woman*" (Gal. 4:26, 31). Galatians 5:1 asserts, "*It is for freedom that Christ has set us free. Stand firm, then, and do not let yourselves be burdened again by a yoke of slavery.*"

This freedom from the law is not just about salvation in heaven but has huge implications for life in the church.

- **Refutation of a Jewish prayer.** Galatians 3:28 probably challenges a Jewish prayer found repeatedly in early Jewish literature: "Blessed art Thou, O Lord our God, King of the Universe, who hast not made me a heathen . . . a bondman . . . [or] a woman."[4] According to rabbinic tradition, these three groups were excluded from the study of Scripture. Paul's denial of these exclusions must therefore require the inclusion of Greeks, slaves, and women in the privilege of studying Scripture.

In summary, Gal. 3:28 is a call to radically new social interactions based on equality in the body of Christ, the church, here on earth. Without any hint that there are exceptions, it states that in Christ there is no male-female division.

NOTES

1. Like the substitution of "whether" (*eite*) in 1 Cor. 12:13.
2. Stephen D. Lowe, "Rethinking the Female Status/Function Question: The Jew/ Gentile Relationship as Paradigm," *JETS* 34 (1991): 59–75.
3. Cf. the references to circumcision in Gal. 2:3, 7, 8, 9, 12; 5:2, 3, 6, 11; 6:12, 13, 15.
4. George S. Duncan, *The Epistle of Paul to the Galatians* (London: Hodder and Stoughton, 1934), 123. This prayer occurs with slight variations in t. Ber. 7.18; b. Menaḥ. 43b (both with "brutish man" for "slave"); y. Ber. 9.1 (136b), 13b (3, 3), 57ff. (7, 2); Cf. also Gen. Rab. 8.9; 22.2; S. Eli. Rab. 7, 10 and 14; Str-B, 3:559–563; Oepke, "γυνή," *TDNT* 1:777 n. 4.

HUSBANDS AND WIVES IN MUTUAL SUBMISSION

Ephesians 5:21–33

"Complementarians" interpret Eph. 5:21–33 to teach "a divinely mandated leadership role for husbands in the marriage relationship and a divinely mandated submission to that leadership for wives . . . in everything."[1] The explicit context of this passage, however, is mutual submission:

> **5:1** Therefore be imitators of God as dearly loved children,
>
> **2** and always walk in love, just as Christ also loved us and gave his life for us, a fragrant offering and sacrifice to God. . . .
>
> **18** Don't get drunk with wine, which leads to reckless indulgence, but be filled with the Spirit,
>
> **19** speaking with one another in psalms, hymns, and spiritual songs, singing and making music from your heart to the Lord,
>
> **20** giving thanks always for everything in the name of our Lord Jesus Christ to God the Father,

21 submitting yourselves to one another out of reverence for Christ, **22** wives to your own husbands as to the Lord, **23** because man is the source of the woman as also Christ is the source of the church, he the savior of the body.[2] **24** Now as the church submits to Christ, in the same way should wives to their husbands in everything.

25 Husbands, always[3] love your wives, just as Christ loved the church and gave his life for her **26** to make her holy, cleansing her by washing her in water with the word, **27** to present to himself the church, brilliant in purity, without stain, wrinkle, or any other flaw, but holy and blameless. **28** In the same way, husbands must love their own wives as they love their own bodies. He who loves his own wife loves himself. **29** After all, no one hates his own flesh, but feeds and tenderly cares for it, just as Christ feeds and tenderly cares for the church **30** because we are members of his body.

31 "This is why a man will leave his father and mother and be united with his wife, and the two will become one flesh."

32 This mystery is profound—but I am speaking about Christ and the church. **33** Nevertheless, as for you, each and every husband must love his wife as himself, and the wife . . . may she respect her husband. (Eph. 5:1–2, 18–33)

Many people focus on "Wives, submit yourselves to your own husbands" without considering its context. In this chapter, Paul calls all Christians to mutual submission and sacrificial love. Ephesians 5:21 is about "submission in the sense of voluntary yielding in love."[4] This includes husbands and wives within their marriages. Paul's words are crafted to fit the Greco-Roman households he addresses. Paul encourages wives to *respect* the man who provides for them food, shelter, clothing, companionship, and love. But this does not exempt them from *loving* their husbands (as 5:2 requires). Husbands then, like husbands today, could be emotionally distant and have their separate worlds. They needed to be told to commit themselves to *love* their wives in practical and active ways, and this applies to husbands today. But this does not exempt them from *respecting* their wives (5:33, cf. 1 Pet. 3:7 *"treat them with respect"*). Although Paul *addresses* specific commands to wives and to husbands, Paul does not give any command here in Ephesians 5 that *applies* only to husbands (and not to wives) or *applies* only to wives (and not to husbands).

In sharp contrast to patriarchal Greco-Roman "household tables," which directly address only the father of the family and assign him final authority in the household, Paul addresses all members of the household and calls all to be accountable to Christ. He tells husbands to love their wives self-sacrificially and masters to treat their slaves justly and with equality (*isotēs*, Col. 4:1). He forbids masters from threatening their slaves and reminds them that there is no favoritism with God (Eph. 6:9; Col. 3:25). These statements by Paul undermine the foundation of Greco-Roman patriarchy—that male masters are superior to females and slaves. Paul's Christ-centered reframing of the "household tables" subverts their Greco-Roman hierarchical purpose.[5]

EPHESIANS 5: ANSWERS TO OBJECTIONS

"But Ephesians 5:22 clearly says that wives are to submit to their husbands."

Originally there was no verb in Eph. 5:22. The earliest manuscripts of Eph. 5:22 (including Vaticanus) do not include the word "submit."[6] The first surviving New Testament manuscript with "submit" in 5:22 (ℵ) was written after AD 350. The missing verb must be implied from Eph. 5:21's "submitting to one another out of reverence for Christ." The command that wives submit to their husbands, therefore, should be understood in the context of mutual submission.

The sentence including Eph. 5:22 actually starts at 5:18. Paul commands all believers, "*Instead, be filled with the Holy Spirit,*" followed by examples of what people do who are filled with the Spirit, concluding with 5:21, "submitting to one another out of reverence for Christ . . ."

Paul states that mutual submission is required of all believers. He continues this sentence in 5:22, "wives to your own husbands" without adding the verb "submit." The NIV paragraph break after verse 21 is in the middle of a sentence. This is not justified. It makes no sense for a new paragraph to begin, "Wives to your own husbands" with no verb. Splitting this sentence into two paragraphs separates "wives to your own husbands" from the context Paul gives it—namely mutual submission.

While Paul calls wives to submit to their husbands here, he makes it clear that the wife's submission is in the context of the mutual submission of believers to each other. I affirm that wives should submit to husbands, but like Paul, I affirm it from within the context of Spirit-filled mutual submission. This context requires that husbands, too, should submit to their wives.

After the section regarding wives and husbands, Paul goes on to address parents and children, then masters and slaves. The paragraph break in some translations between 5:21 and 22 gives another false impression: that verse 21 introduces all three pairs. But Eph. 5:21 is grammatically and verbally linked to 5:22, not to either of the sociological pairs in chapter 6, where Paul uses a different verb, "obey," not "submit."

"But Ephesians 5:23 says the husband is the head of the wife."

The meaning of Paul's closely parallel wording in 1 Cor. 11:3 favors the translation, "because man is the source of the woman (*tēs gynaikos*)." Respect for man as woman's source can motivate a wife to submit. As explained above, pp. 51–58, "authority" was not an established meaning of "head" in the Greek of Paul's day like it is in English, but "source" was. "Source" is also what Paul means by "head" in the prior chapter:

> **15** Instead, speaking the truth in love, we must grow in every respect to be like him who is the head, that is, Christ, **16** from whom the whole body, joined and held together by every supporting ligament, grows and builds itself up in love, as each part does its work. (Eph. 4:15–16)

Here the head is the source "from whom" the body grows. This definition is consistent with other places Paul uses the term, such as:

- "They have lost connection with the head, from whom the whole body, supported and held together by its ligaments and sinews, grows with growth from God" (Col. 2:19).
- "And he is the head of the body, the church, who is its source [*archē*]"[7] (Col. 1:18).

Furthermore, "source" fits how Paul explains "head" in Eph. 5:23. "Head" is in "emphatic apposition" with "savior."[8] As savior, Christ is the source of the church, as Paul explains in verse 25: Christ "*gave himself up for her.*" Similarly, the husband, in that culture, was the source of life for his wife since he provided all that was essential for her to live. "Head" is a natural metaphor for "source" because the head is the source from which the body receives nourishment, breath, sight, hearing, smelling, and taste. This Ephesians passage goes on to command husbands to love, give themselves for (5:25), nourish, and cherish their wives just as Christ does for the church (5:29). Nowhere does it say that husbands have authority over their wives. Paul applies "*submit to one another*" first to wives in verses 22–24 and then to husbands in verses 25–33.

"But the husband is told to love his wife—the wife is not told to love her husband. Furthermore, Christ is the model for the husband only, not his wife."

Neither allegation is true. In Eph. 5:2, Paul commands all believers—including wives—in identical words—what he commands husbands in 5:25: "*Love . . . as Christ loved . . . and gave himself up for us*" (*kathōs kai ho Christos ēgapēsen . . . kai heauton paredōken hyper hymōn*). Additionally, Paul writes that wives should "*love their husbands*" in Titus 2:4. The Bible never teaches that wives are to respect but not love their husbands, or that husbands are to love but not respect their wives.

"But isn't Paul teaching the hierarchy of Christ over the church and making that the model of a husband's hierarchy over his wife?"

This passage highlights Christ's love and self-giving, not Christ's authority. It does not teach any husband-over-wife hierarchy. The relationship between Christ and the church teaches how much love Christ has for the church, and therefore how much love husbands should have for their wives. The key point of the analogy Paul stresses is "love your wives as Christ loved the church" (5:25, 28 twice, 29, 33), not that the husband has authority over his wife, and certainly not that the husband's authority corresponds in any way to the authority Christ has over the church. That would be like deifying husbands! Eph. 5:32, "This mystery is profound—but I am speaking about Christ and the church" expresses the mystery of Paul's analogy. He concludes in verse 33 with his key points, that "every husband must love his wife as himself" and his desire that the wife "respect her husband."

"But Paul specifically commands children to submit to their parents and slaves to submit to their masters. Just as Paul is not trying to eliminate parents' authority over their children, Paul is not trying to eliminate the authority of husbands over their wives."

The NIV's misleading paragraph break between verses 5:21 and 22 gives the false impression that 21a introduces the three following social pairs. Remember that there is no verb in Eph. 5:22—it gets its verb from 5:21's "submitting to one another."

Ephesians affirms mutual submission in the church and in husband-wife relationships, but not regarding either children or slaves. It is not that mutual submission in the body of Christ has no bearing on parent-child or master-slave relations. Rather, husband and wife, as one flesh, uniquely demonstrate the oneness of mutual submission. Consequently, Paul did not need to write "submit" in verse 22. The mutual submission just mentioned in verse 21 applies perfectly to husbands and wives. The following passages about children and slaves use a different verb, "obey."

This understanding of the submission of wives to husbands as one aspect of mutual submission fits Paul's following, far more extensive instructions for husbands to love, cherish, and nourish their wives. It was Paul's commands to husbands that were radically countercultural in his day.

"But what about Colossians 3:18's command that wives submit to their husbands in the Lord?"

Colossians 3:18 states, "Wives submit to your husbands in all ways that are appropriate in the Lord." The Greek text has no comma after "husbands." Wives should not submit in ways that are not appropriate in the Lord, such as Sapphira's collusion with her husband's deceit in Acts 5. The NIV's added comma changes "as is fitting in the Lord" from a restrictive clause into a separate affirmation.

Colossians 3:19 explicitly addresses abuse since it commands husbands not to be harsh with their wives. Harshness has no place in Christian marriage. This passage's introduction, like Gal. 3:28, emphasizes all believers' equal standing:

> Here there is no division between Greek and Jew, circumcised and uncircumcised, barbarian, Scythian, slave and free, but Christ is all and is in all. (Col. 3:11)

Paul teaches that in Christian fellowship there should be no division between slave or free. This undermines slavery.

Colossians 3:5–25 should be interpreted in light of Eph. 5:3–6:9 and its affirmation of mutual submission because of their extensive parallels:

1. Ephesians 5:3–7 parallels Col. 3:5–11's repudiations of sexual immorality and impurity because God's wrath against these is coming.

2. Ephesians 5:19–20 closely parallels Col. 3:16–17:

> *psalms, hymns, and songs from the Spirit. Sing and make music from your heart to the Lord, always giving thanks*

to God the Father for everything in the name of our Lord Jesus Christ. (Eph. 5:19–20)

psalms, hymns, and songs from the Spirit, singing to God with gratitude in your hearts. And whatever you do, whether in word or deed, do it all in the name of the Lord Jesus, giving thanks to God the Father through him. (Col. 3:16–17)

3. Ephesians 5:21–22 makes clear that mutual submission is the context of the command for wives to submit to their husbands. So, too, the "one anothers" of Col. 3:13–16 (*"Bear with each other and forgive one another. . . . Teach and admonish one another"*) affirm mutuality with no gender restriction, as do the central commands to *"clothe yourselves with compassion, kindness, humility, gentleness and patience"* and to *"put on love"* in Col. 3:12, 14. Like mutual submission, "one another" is reciprocal. Furthermore, being taught and accepting admonishment from someone else involves submission. These verses show that Paul has mutual submission in mind. Since both are letters from Paul, we should not interpret Colossians to conflict with his fuller statements regarding mutual submission in Ephesians and 1 Corinthians 7.

4. Ephesians 5:22–6:9 closely parallels the wording of Col. 3:18–4:1:

   18 Wives, submit yourselves to your husbands, in all ways that are appropriate in the Lord.

   19 Husbands, love your wives, and do not be harsh toward them.

20 Children, obey your parents in all things, for this pleases the Lord.

21 Fathers, do not provoke your children, lest they become discouraged.

22 Slaves, in all things obey those who according to earthly standard are your masters, not only when their eye is on you, as people-pleasers, but with a sincere heart fearing the Lord. **23** Whatever you do, do it with your whole heart, as though you were doing it for the Lord, not for human masters, **24** since you know that you will receive an inheritance from the Lord as your reward. Make the Lord Christ the one you serve. **25** For the one who commits injustice will be repaid for that injustice, and there is no favoritism.

4:1 Masters, give justice and equality to your slaves, because you know that you also have a Master in heaven. (Col. 3:18–4:1)

5. Both Col. 3:25 and Eph. 6:9 conclude, "*There is no favoritism.*" So both the introduction and conclusion of these passages emphasize the equal standing of all who are in Christ. Consequently, the submission of wives to husbands in Colossians 3, as in Ephesians 5, is in the context of Christ-centered love for one another.

Thus, like every other call for wives to submit, Col. 3:18's is within the context of mutual submission (Ephesians 5; 1 Peter 3) or to advance the gospel (Titus 2:5; 1 Pet. 3:1).

Why Does This Matter?

I grew up in a home where Dad was the head of the house. Although we all had input on family decisions, Dad made the final decisions. As far as I could tell, this worked out great. I had a wonderful time growing up. Dad treated us to thousands of adventures visiting exotic and memorable places and people all over the world. My father was not just a great dad. J. Barton Payne was also an outstanding Bible scholar who knew all the Semitic languages well. In family devotions, while reading a chapter around the table after breakfast and dinner, when it was his turn, he would always give us a fresh translation directly from the Hebrew or Greek text. I have no recollection of his stumbling over the translation of any word in any verse of Scripture. Dad taught Semitic languages at Princeton, and later at Bob Jones, Wheaton, Trinity Evangelical Divinity School, and Covenant Seminary. He was one of the founders and later president of the Evangelical Theological Society. When I shared what I discovered about women in ministry, he affirmed my findings and showed me how women were approved by God in leadership positions throughout the Hebrew Scriptures as well. Largely because of my home experiences and what I was taught in church, long after I had become convinced that God places no restrictions on the ministry of women, I still thought of myself as the head of my own household.

It was only after I researched how "head" was translated in the Greek Bible that I realized that Paul almost certainly did not use "head" to mean "leader" in Ephesians 5 or anywhere else.[9] I cannot claim that the Bible teaches that I am the "head" of my house.

Looking back, it is now glaringly obvious that I would have

been spared from some of the worst decisions of my life if I had not thought of myself as the "head" of our family but had submitted myself to my wife and her wisdom. Nancy, too, acknowledges that she now wishes she had consulted with me first about some decisions she made. If you think you're the exception who does not need to be answerable to your spouse, just imagine what your life would be like if your spouse had final say over all your decisions. Some people think that someone has to make the final decision, so why shouldn't it be the father? Just think of fathers—or mothers— you know who have made choices without the blessing of their spouse that have burdened them both, sometimes with debt. Wouldn't it have been better for them to have collaborated with each other and avoided that burden?

I didn't know how serious the consequences could be when fathers assume the right to do what they choose as head of the house until Dad and Mom were visiting us while we were missionaries in Japan. For months Dad had been lecturing in seminaries in India, Korea, and Japan, and he was eager to climb Mt. Fuji, as he had climbed Mount Whitney, Mount Olympus, and many other mountains. The only day he could do this was the day we moved from Tokyo to Kyoto, but it was a miserable, rainy day. Mom, Nancy, and I pleaded with Dad not to go, but he was adamant. I remember his words, "I won't cause anyone any trouble, and I'll see you in Kyoto." But he did not arrive in Kyoto on the promised day or the next day. I called the seminaries where he had been teaching, and many of their faculty and students went to Mt. Fuji to search for Barton. The mountain climber who led a search party of seminary students experienced a leg muscle cramp far up the mountain. So they spread out while he rested. Only because of that cramp were they able to find Dad's body. I joined the team the next day and helped carry Dad's body back. I had lost my beloved father, and Christians worldwide had lost one of their most brilliant biblical scholars.

Dad died on Mount Fuji because he believed that he, as head of his wife, had the right to do as he chose with no obligation to submit to his wife. A proper understanding of Ephesians 5 and 1 Cor. 7:4–5—namely, the mutual submission of spouses rather than male headship—could have saved my Dad from death on Mt. Fuji. In marriage as in life, two heads are better than one.

NOTES

1. George W. Knight III, "Husbands and Wives as Analogues of Christ and the Church: Ephesians 5:21–33 and Colossians 3:18–19," in *Recovering Biblical Manhood*, 165–78, at 177, 174.
2. This reflects the Greek wording: "Because man (*anēr*) is the head [as source] of the woman, as also Christ [is] the head [as source] of the church, he the savior of the body." This wording closely parallels 1 Cor. 11:3, where "head" means "source" and *anēr* means "man," as argued above, pp. 52–58. Paul explains that Christ as head/source is the savior of the church (5:23) and that Christ did this by giving his life to bring the church into existence (5:25). Contrary to most translations, Paul did not write, "*The* husband" is head-source of "*his* wife." If Paul had put an article ("the") before "man" and a possessive pronoun ("his") before "woman," I would have translated 5:23: "For the husband (*anēr*) is a source of love and nourishment for his wife as Christ is a source of love and nourishment for the church, he the savior of the body."
3. This is a present imperative, and the aspect of the present shows that this is an ongoing command.
4. BDAG 1042 1.b.β.
5. Argued in detail by Beth Allison Barr, *The Making of Biblical Womanhood: How the Subjugation of Women Became Gospel Truth* (Grand Rapids: Baker, 2021), 45–55.
6. 𝔓⁴⁶ and Codex Vaticanus do not include "submit," nor do its citations by Clement of Alexandria (*Stromata* 4.8.64), Origen, and Theodore of Mopsuestia.

Jerome even writes that in Greek manuscripts verse 22 never repeats the verb "submit" from verse 21. Virtually all editions of the Greek New Testament omit "submit": NA, UBS, Nestle, Westcott-Hort, Tasker, Souter, Alford, Tischendorf. The inclusion of "submit" in Dirk Jongkind et al., eds., *The Greek New Testament Produced at Tyndale House Cambridge* (Cambridge: Cambridge University Press/ Wheaton, IL: Crossway, 2017) is inconsistent with its aim "to present the New Testament books in the earliest form in which they are well attested," p. vii. The United Bible Societies' text ranks the omission of "submit" as "almost certain" (UBS[4] [1998], 3*; UBS[5] [2014], 8*). The view that "submit" was originally in the text and that the earliest manuscripts of this passage and citations of it removed "submit" must not be true, because once "submit" was added to the text, no scribe ever removed it.

7. The earliest manuscripts' detailed apposition: "He is the head . . . who is the source" (*autos estin hē kephalē . . . hos estin hē archē*) explains that "head" means "the source of the body's life" (TEV) or "origin" (NEB). These manuscripts have no punctuation separating "he is the head" from "who is the source." The immediately following "the firstborn from the dead" and verse 20's "by making peace through his blood, shed on the cross" identify how Christ became the source of the body's life and so further support this meaning.

8. A. T. Robertson, *A Grammar of the Greek New Testament in the Light of Historical Research* (Nashville: Broadman & Holman, 1934), 399. Here, "savior" has no article ("the"). All references to "Savior" as a title of Christ are in later literature.

9. Philip Barton Payne, "Response" in *Women, Authority & the Bible*, (Alvera Mickelsen, ed.; Downers Grove, IL: InterVarsity 1986), 118–32.

Nine

HUSBANDS AND WIVES IN MUTUAL SUBMISSION

1 Peter 3:1–7

I t is widely acknowledged that Eph. 5:21 teaches mutual sub-mission[1] and that 5:22 continues that teaching. But few have realized how powerfully Peter expresses mutual submission and applies it to both wives and husbands.

In Acts, Luke tells us that after the stoning of Stephen, Christians were persecuted and scattered.

> **1** *And Saul approved of their killing him* [Stephen].
> *On that day a great persecution broke out against the church in Jerusalem, and all except the apostles were scattered throughout Judea and Samaria.* **2** *Godly men buried Stephen and mourned deeply for him.* **3** *But Saul began to destroy the church. Going from house to house, he dragged off both men and women and put them in prison.*
> (Acts 8:1–3)

Peter wrote to exiles living later among non-Christians, and subject to non-Christian authorities, to encourage them during their suffering. Peter knows that life is difficult for Christian exiles. But most of them have no viable alternative, so they are stuck, however dangerous or painful it may be.

> **1** Peter, *an apostle of Jesus Christ,*
>
> *To God's elect, exiles scattered throughout the provinces of Pontus, Galatia, Cappadocia, Asia and Bithynia. . . .* **6** *In all this you greatly rejoice, though now for a little while you may have had to suffer grief in all kinds of trials.* (1 Pet. 1:1, 6)

> **4:12** *Dear friends, do not be surprised at the fiery ordeal that has come on you to test you, as though something strange were happening to you.* **13** *But rejoice inasmuch as you participate in the sufferings of Christ, so that you may be overjoyed when his glory is revealed.* **14** *If you are insulted because of the name of Christ, you are blessed, for the Spirit of glory and of God rests on you.* **15** *If you suffer, it should not be as a murderer or thief or any other kind of criminal, or even as a meddler.* **16** *However, if you suffer as a Christian, do not be ashamed, but praise God that you bear that name.* **17** *For it is time for judgment to begin with God's household; and if it begins with us, what will the outcome be for those who do not obey the gospel of God?* **18** *And,*
>
> *"If it is hard for the righteous to be saved,*
> *what will become of the ungodly and the sinner?"*
>
> **19** *So then, those who suffer according to God's will should commit themselves to their faithful Creator and continue to do good.* (1 Pet. 4:12–19)

Peter encourages them to stay strong in the faith. He gives them hope that if they lead exemplary lives, they may be able to win over unbelievers. Peter specifically commands them for the Lord's sake to submit to every human authority:

2:11 *Dear friends, I urge you, as foreigners and exiles, to abstain from sinful desires, which wage war against your soul.* **12** *Live such good lives among the pagans that, though they accuse you of doing wrong, they may see your good deeds and glorify God on the day he visits us.*

13 *Submit yourselves for the Lord's sake to every human authority: whether to the emperor, as the supreme authority,* **14** *or to governors, who are sent by him to punish those who do wrong and to commend those who do right.* **15** *For it is God's will that by doing good you should silence the ignorant talk of foolish people.* **16** *Live as free people, but do not use your freedom as a cover-up for evil; live as God's slaves.* **17** *Show proper respect to everyone, love the family of believers, fear God, honor the emperor.* (1 Pet. 2:11–17)

Although commanding submission to governing authorities, Peter affirms the believers' freedom (1 Pet. 2:13–16) as God's slaves (2:16). This command to all believers is the first in a series of commands to "submit." The commands that follow are addressed specifically to Christian slaves, wives, and husbands who are living in a pagan society, many with non-Christian masters or husbands. Peter is not describing an ideal Christian community or endorsing the oppressive social structures he mentions. He gives wise directions to the body of Christ to help them survive this time of trial.

First Peter 2:18–25 calls the Christian exiles who are slaves to "submit" to their masters—even harsh, abusive masters. Peter's words speak to a horrible reality. He does not advocate slavery. But he encourages these exiles by reminding them that Christ, too, suffered unjustly and gave us an example to follow.

Peter similarly commands wives, "in the same way submit" to your own husbands:

3:1 In the same way, wives, submit yourselves to your own husbands so that, even if some of them do not obey the word, they may be won over without a word by their wives' conduct, **2** because they observe the fearful purity of your conduct. **3** Your adornment should not be external—braided hair intertwined with gold, or fine clothing. **4** Instead, make yourselves beautiful in your inner heart with something imperishable, a gentle, calm spirit, which has great value in God's sight. **5** For this is the way holy women who hoped in God used to adorn themselves by submitting themselves to their own husbands. **6** Sarah, for example, obeyed Abraham, and called him "master." You have become her children if you do good and do not fear any terror.

The motive Peter states for wives' submission is not the common Greco-Roman belief that women, since they are by nature inferior, ought to be subordinate to men. Rather, he focuses on wives who have unbelieving husbands and urges them to submit to their husbands so that their unbelieving husbands *"may be won over"* to faith in Christ by means of a silent witness. It was precisely wives' belief in Christ, contrary to their husbands' beliefs, that put them at risk. Wives were expected to adopt their husbands' religious beliefs.[2] Nevertheless, Peter makes it clear that his goal is that their husbands might come to faith in Christ. This hope contrasted with the frightening reality when wives were commanded to renounce Christ, so Peter writes, *"You were redeemed from the empty way of life handed down to you from your ancestors"* (1:18). He urges wives, *"Do not fear any terror"* (3:6). First Peter throughout is an appeal to believers who have been tested *"by fire"* (1:7), faced *"abuse"* (4:4) and *"the fiery ordeal"* (4:12), been *"insulted because of the name of Christ"* (4:14). They are to *"endure"*

(2:20) and "*not be ashamed*" as they suffer for the faith (4:13–16), but to "*stand fast*" (5:12), "*firm in the faith*" (5:9).

Wives of abusive husbands and victims of slavery probably did not have any options back then, but they do now. Victims of abuse need to get help and get out! Talk to someone or call for help! One such organization is the National Domestic Violence Hotline at 1–800-799-7233.

Peter next issues commands to husbands who are believers. In this case, he specifically refers to their wives as believers as well. Thus, his commands are distinctively Christian.

Husbands, in the same way submit yourselves to your own wives, dwelling together wisely, recognizing her as a weaker feminine[3] precious vessel, and assign them the honor they deserve as coheirs with you of the gracious gift of life, so that your prayers won't be hindered. (1 Pet. 3:7)

In Greek, this sentence has no main verb, but the command "submit" is implied because "in the same way" demands something parallel to the preceding commands. Each of the three preceding sections begins with a command to "submit" using the same verb, *hypotassō*:

- "**Submit yourselves** *for the Lord's sake to every human authority*" (2:13)
- "*Slaves, in reverent fear of God* **submit yourselves** *to your masters*" (2:18)
- "*Wives, in the same way* [homoiōs] **submit yourselves** *to your own husbands*" (3:1)

So when Peter writes in 3:7, "*Husbands in the same way [homoiōs]* . . . ," the only command supplied by the context is "submit," and "submit" fits the context perfectly.[4] Furthermore, the close parallel between "In the same way [*homoiōs*], wives, submit yourselves to your own husbands" and "Husbands in the same way [*homoiōs*] . . ." naturally implies, "Husbands in the same way [submit yourselves to your own wives]." The NIV translates the prepositional modifier *kata gnōsin* ("according to knowledge," that is, "wisely, recognizing her") as the main verb, *be considerate*. But *kata gnōsin* is not a verb and does not mean "*be considerate*," and no verb like *be considerate* is in any manuscript of 1 Pet. 3:7, nor is there anything similar to it in the preceding context. The context, therefore, clearly supports that 1 Pet. 3:7 means: "Husbands in the same way submit yourselves to your own wives."

1 PETER 3:1–7: ANSWERS TO OBJECTIONS

"What makes you think Peter would honor wives as equal in standing with their husbands?"

Peter's description of the wives as "*heirs with you of the gracious gift of life*" (3:7) shows that he recognizes wives' equal standing in Christ with their husbands. This contrasts sharply with women's unequal and disadvantaged legal position regarding such things as inheritance in Peter's day. Furthermore, "assign them the honor they deserve" uses the Greek noun for "honor" that conveys social status. Peter, therefore, commands the believing husband to grant his wife honor and social status that was exceptional in that culture.

"What makes you think Peter believed in mutuality like this?"

Immediately after writing "Husbands, in the same way [submit to your own wives]," Peter encourages mutuality: "*Be* like-minded, be sympathetic, love one another, be compassionate and humble" (3:7, 8).

The phrase "weaker feminine vessel" may mean that wives tend to be physically weaker than husbands, so the husbands should treat their wives with consideration and respect and not use their strength to their advantage. "Weaker" may also refer to the wife's weaker social position in that culture. The use of "vessel/pottery" with "weaker" and "feminine" in the context of "joint heirs" suggests a fragile, precious vessel. Although women were regarded as weaker than men in that culture, they are precious in God's sight. Indeed, they are full inheritors in Christ.

"*So that nothing will hinder your prayers*" shows that for husbands not to submit themselves to and honor their wives will have serious consequences. It gives God pleasure for husbands to honor their wives as coheirs of the gracious gift of life, treating them as the equals God created them to be. God blesses husband-wife mutual submission.

"Does Sarah's calling Abraham her lord affirm hierarchical marriage?"

The only time Scripture refers to Abraham as Sarah's lord is probably what Peter refers to.[5] It follows, "*Abraham hurried into the tent to Sarah. 'Quick,' he said, 'get three seahs[6] of the finest flour and knead it and bake some bread'*" for the three divine visitors (Gen 18:1–6). After they feast, they predict that Sarah will have a son. Genesis 18:12 records that "*Sarah laughed to herself as she thought, 'After I am worn out and my lord is old, will I now have this pleasure?'*" Sarah was referring to having "pleasure with," namely sexual relations with her husband resulting in the joy of having her own child. Since Sarah conceived Isaac, she must have had sex with Abraham, in obedience to the prophecy and to Abraham. This whole narrative aptly fits Peter's reference to "*Sarah, who obeyed Abraham and called him her lord.*" Furthermore, it is a memorable story and a crucial event in preserving the line of Christ (Matt. 1:2; Luke. 3:34). Peter's reference to this account would have encouraged believing wives not to be afraid to have pleasure with their unbelieving husbands sexually, just as Paul encourages in 1 Cor. 7:3–5. This is practical advice "so that, even if some of them [their husbands] do not obey the word, they may be won over without a word by their wives' conduct" (1 Pet. 3:1).

Both the context in 1 Peter and the Sarah narratives are ill-suited for endorsing hierarchical marriage. Scripture never records God telling Sarah to obey Abraham, but God does tell Abraham to obey Sarah in Gen. 21:12. Abraham also "obeyed" Sarah, using the same word 1 Pet. 3:6 uses for Sarah's obedience in Gen. 16:2 LXX.

In summary, Peter gives guidance to Christians who were exiles in a pagan land. It is striking that just as Paul commands wives and husbands to submit to one another in Eph. 5:21–22, Peter also commands both wives and husbands to submit to their spouses and for husbands to honor their wives as joint heirs of the gracious gift of life (1 Pet. 3:7).

NOTES

1. As even Knight, "Husbands," 166–67.
2. E.g. Plutarch, *Advice to Bride and Groom* 19, *Moralia* 140d (LCL).
3. BDAG 208, *gynaikeios*, "feminine."
4. As Peter H. Davids argues in "A Silent Witness in Marriage: 1 Peter 3:1–7," in *Discovering Biblical Equality*, 228–44, at 243. J. N. D. Kelly also asserts this, but because he believed that husbands "have a natural authority over their wives, it would be inexact to define this as subordination, but the principle requires that they should exercise their authority with proper deference." J. N. D. Kelly, *A Commentary on the Epistles of Peter and Jude* (Grand Rapids: Baker, 1969), 132.
5. It is doubtful that Peter had access to the *Testament of Abraham*. M. R. James, *The Testament of Abraham, the Greek Text now first edited with an Introduction and Notes*

(Cambridge: CUP, 1892), 55, "The Testament was originally put together in the second century by a Jewish Christian." E. P. Sanders, "Testament of Abraham," pages 869–902 in *Old Testament Pseudepigrapha* (ed. J..H. Charlesworth; 2 vols.; Garden City, NY: Doubleday, 1983), 1:869 notes that the *Testament of Abraham* likely comes from the first or second century AD. Furthermore, none of the *Testament of Abraham*'s references to "my *kyrios* Abraham" are in a context of obedience that would explain: "*Sarah, who obeyed Abraham and called him her lord.*"

6. Roughly three bushels. This event also explains Jesus's reference to yeast hidden in three *satah* of flour (Matt. 13:33).

Ten

SEIZING AUTHORITY TO TEACH & "SAVED THROUGH THE CHILDBIRTH"

1 Timothy 2

"Complementarians" widely regard 1 Tim. 2:8–15 as proof that women must not teach or exercise authority over a man. Some read into Eve's deception that women are more easily deceived than men. Because such (mis)understandings of 1 Tim. 2:8–15 contradict Paul's affirmations of women in leadership elsewhere, some Bible scholars conclude that Paul could not have written 1 Timothy. Even many self-identified "complementarians" believe that women can teach and exercise authority over men in some circumstances, particularly in the secular workplace or government, but also as Christian professors, theological authors, and spiritual counselors. So this passage at first glance seems to be difficult for everyone, whether they believe in male hierarchy or equal opportunity for women and men.

Exactly what does this passage teach? First, we should consider why Paul wrote this letter to Timothy.

WHAT PROBLEM DOES PAUL
ADDRESS IN 1 TIMOTHY?

In 1 and 2 Timothy, Paul guides Timothy through a crisis caused
by false teachers in the church in Ephesus. Remember that Paul
helped start the church in Ephesus (Acts 18–20) and warned the
elders when he left:

> **29** I know that after I leave, savage wolves will come in among you
> and will not spare the flock. **30** Even from your own number men will
> arise and distort the truth in order to draw away disciples after them.
> **31** So be on your guard! Remember that for three years I never stopped
> warning each of you night and day with tears. (Acts 20:29–31)

First Timothy's introduction confirms that this letter
addresses false teaching. But Paul differentiates between those
who were false teachers because they were ignorant and those
who were willfully blasphemous. For example, Paul himself was
a false teacher, but he was ignorant, as he confesses:

> Even though I was once a blasphemer and a persecutor and a violent
> man, I was shown mercy because I acted in ignorance and unbelief. . . .
> But for that very reason I was shown mercy so that in me, the worst
> of sinners, Christ Jesus might display his immense patience as an
> example for those who would believe in him and receive eternal life.
> (1 Tim. 1:13, 16)

On the other hand, in 1 Tim. 1:18–20 Paul names two specific teachers in Ephesus who were knowingly spreading false
teachings:

> **18** Timothy, my son, I am giving you this command in keeping with
> the prophecies once made about you, so that by recalling them you
> may fight the battle well, **19** holding on to faith and a good conscience,
> which some have rejected and so have suffered shipwreck with regard
> to the faith. **20** Among them are Hymenaeus and Alexander, whom I
> have handed over to Satan to be taught not to blaspheme.

Those who blaspheme knowingly are to be rejected. The
only two false teachers named in 1 Timothy, Hymenaeus and
Alexander, are men whom Paul has already "*handed over to Satan*"
(1 Tim. 1:20). But the rest of the first half of 1 Timothy deals with
those who had been deceived by the false teachers and were
spreading those false teachings out of ignorance. These misin-
formed teachers were not knowingly spreading false teachings.
They were deceived in their ignorance, as Paul had been.

But how do we know that women were involved in continuing
the false teaching?

First, whenever in 1 Timothy Paul describes the false teachers collectively, he consistently uses the Greek word *tis* (meaning
"someone" or "anyone"), for example:

> Stay there in Ephesus . . . that you may command certain people [tis]
> not to teach false doctrines. (1:3)

> Some [tis] have departed from these and have turned to meaningless
> talk. (1:6)

> I am giving you this command . . . so that . . . you may fight the battle
> well, holding on to faith and a good conscience, which some [tis] have
> rejected. (1:18–19)

If the false teachers were only men, then we would have expected Paul to use masculine terms to describe them. Paul's use of this inclusive term suggests that some false teachers were women.

Furthermore, Paul uses parallel expressions to describe both the false teachers and specific women. For example, Paul mentions that some false teachers have turned to meaningless talk, and later he mentions that some women talk nonsense:

> *Some have departed from these and have turned to meaningless talk.*
> (1:6)

> [Younger widows] *become idlers, but also busybodies who talk nonsense, saying things they ought not to.* (5:13)

Also, some false teachers abandoned the faith and followed demonic teachings; and later Paul mentions some women who swerved from their first faith and turned to follow Satan:

> *The Spirit clearly says that in later times some will abandon the faith and follow deceiving spirits and things taught by demons.* (4:1)

> *Thus they* [younger widows] *bring judgment on themselves, because they have swerved from their first faith.* (5:12)

> *Some* [younger widows] *have in fact already turned away to follow Satan.* (5:15)

Then in 2 Timothy, Paul refers to women who were misled. They are probably some of the women Paul refers to in 1 Timothy:

6 *They are the kind who worm their way into homes and gain control over vulnerable women, who are loaded down with sins and are swayed by all kinds of evil desires,* **7** *always learning but never able to come to a knowledge of the truth.* (2 Tim. 3:6–7)

Finally, remember from Acts 19 that Ephesus was the center for worship of the Greek goddess Artemis (the goddess of protection during childbirth). The people were lured by promises of protection during pregnancy and childbirth. Many leaders of this cult were women. Therefore, followers of Artemis who joined the church would expect that women could lead.

The church at Ephesus had a serious problem with false teachers. Following Paul's judgment on the original false teachers, the only people 1 Timothy identifies as deceived by the false teachings are women. Paul had earlier instructed Timothy to *"command certain people not to teach false doctrines any longer"* (1 Tim. 1:3). But the women who had been deceived by the false teaching should learn (2:11), and Timothy should be patient with them as Christ was with Paul.

DON'T FORGET PRISCILLA

We are about to talk about verses that many people think prohibit women from teaching men. Before we do that, I want you to think about Priscilla. Remember that Paul met Priscilla and her husband, Aquila, in Corinth, and they all worked together:

1 *After this, Paul left Athens and went to Corinth.* **2** *There he met a Jew named Aquila, a native of Pontus, who had recently come from Italy with his wife Priscilla, because Claudius had ordered all Jews to* leave Rome. Paul went to see them, **3** and because he was a tentmaker as they were, he stayed and worked with them. (Acts 18:1–3)

Later on, when Paul left Corinth, Priscilla and Aquila went with him. Together, they went to Ephesus:

18 Paul stayed on in Corinth for some time. Then he left the brothers and sisters and sailed for Syria, accompanied by Priscilla and Aquila. Before he sailed, he had his hair cut off at Cenchreae because of a vow he had taken. **19** They arrived at Ephesus, where Paul left Priscilla and Aquila. He himself went into the synagogue and reasoned with the Jews. (Acts 18:18–19)

That's right, Priscilla and Aquila are in Ephesus, the same city where Timothy faces a crisis of false teaching. They are teaching people in Ephesus about Jesus.

24 Meanwhile a Jew named Apollos, a native of Alexandria, came to Ephesus. He was a learned man, with a thorough knowledge of the Scriptures. **25** He had been instructed in the way of the Lord, and he spoke with great fervor and taught about Jesus accurately, though he knew only the baptism of John. **26** He began to speak boldly in the synagogue. When Priscilla and Aquila heard him, they took him aside and explained to him the way of God more adequately. (Acts 18:24–26. Note that the Greek text states simply, "they took him aside" (cf. BDAG 883). The NIV incorrectly translates this, "they invited him to their home." Since "took him aside" is not the NIV text, it is not italicized.)

Since Priscilla's name is mentioned first here, contrary to normal Greek convention and to their introduction in Acts 18:2, it is reasonable to infer that she did at least some of this biblical teaching, and probably most of it—to a man—a dynamic preacher *with a thorough knowledge of the Scriptures* (Acts 18:24). Some people say she did not "teach" a man but only *"explained to him the way of God more adequately"* or "more accurately" (NASB), but if "explaining the way of God more accurately" is not teaching, what is? Others say that she could only do this because her husband was with her, but no Bible passage says a woman can teach only if her husband is with her. Still others say that because she was teaching just one man, this is different from what 1 Tim. 2:12 prohibits, but 1 Tim. 2:12 also specifies "to teach . . . a man" (singular). Apparently Priscilla had returned to Ephesus from Rome (Rom. 16:3) before Paul wrote 2 Timothy because Paul writes in 2 Tim. 4:19, "Greet Prisca and Aquila." Paul gives her special respect by listing her name first and using the respectful form of her name, as Paul always does. Priscilla was probably Timothy's best resource to correct deceived women in Ephesus. If she was in Ephesus when Paul wrote 1 Timothy, it is doubtful that Paul would silence his best resource. Keep this in mind as we dive deeper into 1 Timothy.

DEALING WITH THE PROBLEM (1 TIM. 2:8–12)

False teachers had infiltrated the church at Ephesus, just as Paul had warned them in Acts 20. How should Timothy deal with those who had been deceived by the false teachers? Keep in mind that the women spreading these false teachings were doing so in ignorance, not willfully deceiving others. The first step is to make sure they have the right mindset: humility before God.

8 Therefore I want the men in every place to pray, lifting up holy hands without anger or quarrelling. **9** Similarly, I want women to pray in appropriate clothing, to adorn themselves with modesty and self-control, not with hair braided with gold, or pearls or lavish clothing, **10** but with what is appropriate for women who profess reverence for God—good deeds.

(1 Tim. 2:8–10)

Some translations make it sound as if Paul wants men to pray, but women only to dress modestly. However, Paul probably didn't intend this. Verse 9 starts with the Greek word *hōsautōs*, which means "similarly." All sixteen instances of *hōsautōs* in the New Testament show obvious close parallels between the two statements compared, most of them in multiple details. In every other instance where the verb in the sentence preceding *hosautos* fits the *hōsautōs* clause, readers transfer that verb (here, "pray") to the *hōsautōs* clause. Likewise, verse 8 tells men what is improper when they pray, and *hōsautōs* introducing verse 9 similarly tells women what is improper when they pray. Unfortunately, the NIV not only mistranslates "similarly" as "also," it fails to convey any similarity.

Paul next addresses the fundamental problem of women who are not properly trained:

A woman must learn in a calm manner and in full submission.

(1 Tim. 2:11)

"Learn" here is imperative. Paul commands that women must learn. He is not merely giving advice about the manner in which women should learn. This is the only imperative verb in this chapter. The sense of "calm" parallels 1 Tim. 2:2's *"peaceful and quiet lives"* and uses the same root word. The word for "silence" in 1 Cor. 14:28, 34 is different. Since "in a calm manner" modifies "learn," its parallel "in full submission" must also modify "learn."

Full submission to the teaching is the key to counteract the false teaching. Paul commands submission, not to male teachers, but to sound teaching, which may have been given by Priscilla.

But you may ask, "Why does Paul command this of women, not men?" Because the context indicates that women were perpetuating the main problem Paul addresses. And there was already a culture of men learning from rabbis—but there was no established convention for how women should learn.

Next, we come to arguably the most controversial verse on the topic of women and teaching:

> [In light of the crisis of false teaching,] I am not permitting
> a woman to seize authority to teach a man, but to be calm.
> (1 Tim. 2:12)

We will go through it carefully. There are four points to consider about this sentence:

First, the verb in the phrase "*I am not permitting*" is a present active indicative verb in the Greek. This indicates something that is presently ongoing, so is better translated, "I am not permitting." In grammatical studies, this is called the "aspect" of the present. It does not imply a permanent state or a universal command like the NIV's "*I do not permit*" does.

Second, this verb, "*permit*," is never used in the original text of the Bible as a universal command,[1] but instead indicates temporary permission for a specific situation, as in the following verses:

> *He ordered the centurion to keep Paul under guard but to give him*
> *some freedom and permit his friends to take care of his needs.*
> (Acts 24:23)

For I do not want to see you now and make only a passing visit; I hope
to spend some time with you, if the Lord permits. (1 Cor. 16:7)

Therefore let us move beyond the elementary teachings about Christ
and be taken forward to maturity. . . . And God permitting, we will
do so. (Heb. 6:1–3)

Paul uses many imperatives, but "I am not permitting" is not
an imperative, and Paul's original letters don't use the verb "permit" to give a permanent command.

Third, the word translated "*to assume authority*" is *authentein.*
Normally, we would begin by examining how the Bible uses this
word elsewhere to help us understand its usage here. However,
the Bible never uses this word elsewhere. It consists of two other
words: *autos* (meaning "by oneself, of one's own initiative," as in
"autobiography"), and *hentes* (meaning "who finishes, achieves").[2]
The word stresses the activity of the self, as in "accomplish
for one's own advantage."[3] It has a common nuance of acting
unilaterally—like "autocrat."[4] Related words usually convey a
negative nuance. The most common meaning of this word around
Paul's time was "to assume authority that one does not rightfully have."[5]

In 2010 I submitted to the committee chairmen of the NIV
and ESV revision committees research documenting the use of
this verb around the time of Paul to mean "to assume authority
that one does not rightfully have." It showed that the first clear
instance of *authentein* meaning "to exercise authority" was from
ca. AD 370 in Saint Basil.[6] Doug Moo, the chairman of the NIV
revision committee, provided my research to the committee for
consideration and discussion. I still remember the day Dr. Moo

phoned me to say, "The NIV revision committee has chosen to adopt your recommended translation, 'to assume authority,' which replaced the former NIV translation 'to have authority.'" This is a refreshing example of a leading "complementarian" not only considering evidence provided by an egalitarian, but giving that evidence to the committee with the authority to change the NIV text. The fact that the committee, which included many other "complementarians," adopted the change shows how powerful the evidence is for that change. In contrast, the ESV revision committee chairman did not even let his committee see my recommended changes.

Fourth, the two verbs here, "*to teach*" and "*to assume authority*," are joined by the coordinating conjunction *oude* to prohibit the *combination* of teaching and assuming authority, just like Origen explained.[7] We discussed this word in Gal. 3:28. Likewise here, Paul is not talking about two separate issues, "teaching" and "assuming authority," but about their combination: "assuming authority to teach." In other words, Paul is not prohibiting two separate actions—he is prohibiting the *combination* of teaching and assuming authority.

Let's put those four points together: in the currently ongoing crisis of false teaching in Ephesus, Paul is not permitting women to assume authority to teach if they do not have that authority. Priscilla, who had recognized authority to teach (Acts 18:26) and whom Paul greets in this same city in 2 Tim. 4:19, would not be assuming authority to teach since she already had that recognized authority. She would have been a key resource to Timothy because she could correct women deceived by false teachings. And finally, do not forget that the one and only imperative in this passage is "A woman must learn" (1 Tim. 2:11 NET).

1 TIMOTHY 2:
ANSWER TO THE MOST COMMON OBJECTION

"Why would Paul specifically limit a woman from assuming author-ity to teach a man?"

Paul does not explain this, but this wording makes sense because Timothy could not monitor what women were teaching other women privately. Prohibiting a woman specifically from assuming authority to teach "a man," however, addressed what would occur at typical public church meetings that Timothy could monitor. Paul's specification of "a man" made this a limited and crystal-clear rule (unlike prohibiting "false doctrine," since people almost always think that what they teach is true, so they would deny that they taught "false doctrine") that Timothy could enforce without offending cultural standards of privacy. This specification of "teach a man" was also practical because false teaching would spread most quickly in public meetings of the church (where a man would presumably be present) and could give the church a bad reputation.

BACK TO THE GARDEN (1 TIM. 2:13–15)

After telling Timothy that women must not assume authority to teach, if they do not have that authority, but instead should learn, Paul goes on in 1 Tim. 2:13–15 to justify his restriction:

> **13** For Adam was formed first, then Eve was formed. **14** And Adam was not deceived, but the woman, being thoroughly deceived, fell into transgression. **15** But anyone will be saved through the birth of Jesus if they continue in faith, love and holiness with self-control.

Since woman was formed out of man, she should respect man as her source, just as 1 Cor. 11:3, 8 and 12 explain.[8] It was disrespectful for a woman to seize authority to teach a man. "Then Eve" is the first documented affirmation that Eve was "formed" by God. With these words, Paul affirms the essential equality of men and women.

Many people interpret "the woman, being thoroughly deceived" to mean that women should not be leaders because women are more easily deceived than men. A review of Adam's behavior in the garden of Eden, however, lets us see this passage in a new light. Genesis does not mention Adam during the conversation between the serpent and the woman in Gen. 3:1–5. The text does not imply—and certainly does not state—that the serpent's conversation with the woman occurred at the tree of the knowledge of good and evil. Only Gen. 3:6 states that her husband *"was with her"* at that tree. To be deceived, someone must be convinced to believe something that is not true. If Adam heard (or overheard) the serpent's deceptive words and believed them, then he, too, was deceived by the serpent. If not, he was not deceived by the serpent. This may explain why Paul says that Adam was not deceived. But still, Adam disobeyed God's command. Remember what happened:

She also gave some to her husband, who was with her, and he ate it.
(Gen. 3:6)

She gave him the fruit—he knew which tree it came from—and he ate it. Unless there was some other conversation that the text does not mention, his eating the forbidden fruit does not even rise to the level of "deception"—it is simply disobedience. What Adam did was just dumb for someone God had told, *"When you eat from it you will certainly die"* (2:17). Then when God confronted

Adam, he passed the buck, blaming both the woman and, implicitly, God: "*The woman you put here with me—she gave me some fruit from the tree, and I ate it*" (3:12). There is nothing that Adam does here that is honorable in any way. Nothing worthy of imitating or saying, "Sorry, women, we need more leaders like Adam."

When Paul says that "*Adam was not the one deceived*" (1 Tim. 2:14), Paul does not declare Adam innocent and certainly does not suggest that he is morally superior. So what does Paul mean? The serpent did not speak to Adam—Paul highlights the fact that Adam was not the target of Satan's deception. The passive voice of the verb in "the woman who was thoroughly deceived [*exapate‾theisa*]" implies that the serpent deceived her. It makes it clear that the serpent, Satan, targeted the woman and deceived her into disobeying God's command.

Can you think of any more powerful example of the danger deceived women pose to the church than Eve's deception? Consider the immediate context in Ephesus. Women were deceived and were passing on their deception, just as happened in the garden of Eden. Paul's solution is clear. "Let the women learn" so they can become teachers who are not easily deceived.

There have been numerous attempts to explain the meaning of "shall be saved through the childbirth" (2:15). Each of the three occurrences of "childbirth" in Greek literature prior to Paul refer to the birth of a child, not the process of childbearing. "The childbirth" has an article, so Paul says women will be saved through "the childbirth." Of the sixty-one occurrences of an article with a singular noun in 1 Timothy, fifty-five are clearly individualizing, and only one is clearly generic (1 Tim. 4:8). Therefore, Paul probably intended one specific childbirth.

Every other instance of any word related to "save" (*sōzō*) in Paul's letters regards spiritual salvation, and this fits the conditions that follow: "If they continue in faith, love and holiness." What childbirth saves? The only child ever born who can save anybody was Jesus. Indeed, Paul had just written, "Christ Jesus came into the world to save sinners" (1:15) and shortly thereafter writes, "He appeared in the flesh" (3:16). Paul similarly expresses the means of salvation using the passive of *sōzō* with *dia* + genitive "saved through the gospel" in 1 Cor. 15:2.

Paul wrote seven letters with his emissary Timothy (Romans, 2 Corinthians, Philippians, Colossians, 1–2 Thessalonians, Philemon). Timothy could recognize Christ as the promised "seed of the woman" (Gen. 3:15; cf. Gal. 3:16). This encourages and empowers women. This sentence does not teach that "women should stay home and make babies." It is best translated, "But anyone will be saved through the birth of Jesus if they continue in faith, love and holiness with self-control."

NOTES

1. See the evidence above, pp. 79–101 and 185–89, that 1 Cor. 14:34–35 was not in Paul's original letter.
2. See LSJ 275, "(cf. αὐτοέντης) murderer, Hdt. 1.117, E.Rh.873; Th.3.58 . . . (For αὐτο-έντης, cf. συν-έντης, ἀνύω; root sen–, sn̥–.)"; Payne, *Man and Woman, One in Christ*, 363–65.
3. LSJ 168.
4. Pierre Chantraine, *Dictionnaire étymologique de la Langue Grecque: Histoire des Mots* (4 vols. Paris: Klincksieck, 1968–1980) 1:138–9.
5. Demonstrated in Payne, *Man and Woman, One in Christ*, 361–97.
6. *The Letters* 69, line 45.
7. C. Jenkins, "Documents: Origen on 1 Corinthians. IV," JTS 10 (1909): 29–51, at 42. Philip B. Payne, "1 Timothy 2.12 and the Use of οὐδέ [oude] to Combine Two Elements to Express a Single Idea," NTS 54 (2008): 235–53, at 246. Philip B. Payne, "Οὐδέ [oude] Combining Two Elements to Convey a Single Idea and 1 Timothy 2:12," in *Missing Voices: Broadening the Discussion on Men, Women, and Ministry*, ed. Hilary Ritchie (Minneapolis: CBE International, 2014), 24–34, at 25. Parallel structures (not X oude Y but Z) regularly join two elements to convey a single idea.

8. Cf. above, pp. 51–58, 64, 66–67, 70–71, and Philo QG 1.27.

9. Neither "*will be saved*" nor "*if they continue*" is feminine in gender, nor does either have a feminine pronoun as subject. Since everything in this sentence applies equally well to all believers, the assumed subject "anyone" best fits the shift from singular ("anyone will be saved") to plural ("if they continue"). Dorothy A. Lee, *The Ministry of Women in the New Testament: Reclaiming the Biblical Vision for Church Leadership* (Grand Rapids: Baker, 2021), 128, also argues for the translation: "will be saved through the Childbirth, if they . . ."

Eleven

OVERSEER AND DEACON QUALIFICATIONS

1 Timothy 3

OVERSEER QUALIFICATIONS (1 TIMOTHY 3:1–7)

3:1 Here is a trustworthy saying: Anyone who aspires to the office of overseer desires a beneficial task. **2** The overseer, therefore, must be exemplary, devoted to one spouse if married, sober, self-controlled, worthy of respect, hospitable to everyone, a good teacher, **3** not a heavy drinker or a bully, but gentle, peaceable, not materialistic, **4** who takes good care of their own home, whose children (if they have any) are obedient and respectful **5** (for how can anyone who doesn't take care of their own home take care of God's church?), **6** not a new convert, so that they won't become conceited and fall into the devil's judgment. **7** An overseer must also have a good reputation beyond the church, to avoid public humiliation and the devil's trap. (1 Tim. 3:1–7)

When Paul writes "anyone" in 3:1, he uses the Greek word tis, which is inclusive and gender-neutral. It would be misleading to use *tis* without qualification to describe a group limited to males. Furthermore, the preceding passage is about men and women. Paul had men and women in mind. If Paul had intended to teach that only men should be overseers, he would have said something like, "Any *man* who aspires to the office of overseer desires a noble task." But Paul does not say "man." Paul says "anyone" because Paul means "anyone"—man or woman. Nevertheless, of the sixty-two Bible translations on Biblegateway.com, twenty-one insert "man" plus a masculine pronoun ("he" or "him") into 3:1, including the KJV and NASB, and twenty-three more insert one or more masculine pronouns into 3:1, including the ESV and RSV. The CEV and CEB accurately reflect the Greek by having no "he," "him," or "his" in Paul's qualifications for overseer in 1 Tim. 3:1–7 and for elder in Titus 1:5–9. Most translations, however, add many of these masculine pronouns to these paragraphs.

What, then, is left to restrict women from becoming overseers? Well, the word for "the overseer" in 3:2 is a masculine noun, but it's simply Greek convention when groups of people are addressed to use masculine grammatical forms. Timothy Friberg counted between 7,500 and 8,000 grammatically masculine forms in the New Testament, almost one per sentence, that either must or could include women. Accordingly, merely the presence of one or more masculine nouns or adjectives cannot legitimately be used to exclude women from this text or any other passage about a group of people.

Greek nouns are assigned to one of three genders—masculine, feminine, and neuter. "The masculine is used in speaking of persons *generally*, even when only women are in view: as in Acts 9:37 ["washed"], Mark 5:38 ["weeping" {and "wailing loudly"}]. . . . There is no *necessary* connection between sex and gender."[1] "Head," "the office of overseer," and "testicle" are grammatically feminine nouns. "Child" is neuter.

This leaves us with only one expression in this paragraph that some have interpreted to exclude women. Paul says that an overseer must be a "man of one woman" (*mias gynaikos andra*). It is typically translated "*faithful to his wife.*" The closest English equivalent word is "monogamous," which can refer to either men or women. The word here for "man" typically does mean "man," though it can also mean "person."[2] Since here it is combined with "of one woman," it naturally means "man." That by itself, however, does not limit overseers to married men for three reasons.

First, the apostle Paul oversaw the churches he planted, but, like Jesus, he was single and encouraged both men and women to lead a single life of devotion to the Lord (1 Cor. 7:7–8, 32–35). Consequently, it is not credible that Paul would debar single people from being local church overseers. Thus, "man of one woman" must not require that all overseers be married men. It requires only that *if* a man is married, he must be faithful to his wife, as John Chrysostom explains.[3]

Second, it is common in both Hebrew and Greek for rules to address men with the assumption that the rule also applies to women. For example, in the ten commandments, "*You shall not covet your neighbor's wife*" (Ex. 20:17; Deut. 5:21; cf. Mal. 2:15) also applies to wives coveting their neighbor's husband. Gordon Hugenberger states, "In the absence of other constraints, norms that utilize male-oriented terminology ought to be construed in general as including both sexes in their purview."[4] Accordingly, John Chrysostom writes regarding this phrase in 1 Tim. 3:12, "Deacons must be men of one woman. This is appropriate to say regarding women deacons also."[5] Even prominent "complementarian" scholars, including Thomas Schreiner and Doug Moo, acknowledge that "man of one woman" does not exclude women from the office of overseer.[6]

Third, "man of one woman" is an idiom. None of the three Greek words by itself means "*faithful.*" It is only the combination of the three words that together mean "*faithful.*" Those three words are a figure of speech, an idiom. They act like a noun. And like many Greek nouns, it comes in masculine and feminine forms. Greek convention uses masculine forms when describing both men and women, as here.

But this idiom also comes in a feminine form. Paul uses this feminine form later in chapter 5 when describing which widows should receive assistance. First Timothy 5:9 requires that the widow must have been "*faithful to her husband.*" Paul uses the feminine form of the idiom, "woman of one man" (*henos andros gynē*), because "widows" are exclusively female.

So when Paul tells Timothy that overseers should be faithful people, he could choose either the masculine or feminine form of the idiom. There is no gender-neutral form of the idiom such as "spouse of one spouse." Convention, however, required the masculine form of the idiom when referring to a group of people who might be either men or women. The feminine form was only used when the group is exclusively female. Consequently, the idiomatic phrase "man of one woman" *includes* men as potential overseers; it does not *exclude* women.

In summary, Paul begins these requirements with his thesis statement: "Anyone who aspires to the office of overseer desires a beneficial task." This encourages women to aspire to the office of overseer, and nothing else in this paragraph overrules that. None of the qualifications exclude women.

DEACON QUALIFICATIONS (1 TIM. 3:8–13)

Following these overseer qualifications, Paul lists qualifications for the office of deacon:

> **8** Deacons, similarly, must be worthy of respect, sincere, neither indulging in much wine nor being greedy, **9** holding on to the astounding truth of the faith with a clear conscience. **10** They must first be evaluated, and if they pass the test, then serve as deacons. **11** In just the same way, women who are deacons must be worthy of respect, not slanderers, but sober and faithful in everything. **12** Married deacons must be devoted to their spouse and take good care of their children and their home. **13** For those who have served well as deacons gain good standing for themselves and great confidence in their faith in Christ Jesus. (1 Tim. 3:8–13)

Paul begins both verse 8 and verse 11, "Deacons, similarly (*hōsautōs*) . . ." to cause readers to add the implied compound verb "it is necessary for [deacons] to be" from verse 2. Verse 8 identifies four requirements: "worthy of respect, sincere, neither indulging in much wine nor being greedy."

Since there is no corresponding "anyone" in 3:8–10, to make it clear that women can be deacons, too, Paul repeats in verse 11 essentially these same four qualifications in the same order for women deacons: "worthy of respect, not slanderers, but sober and faithful in everything." This combined with "similarly" (*hōsautōs*) makes it clear that both verses 8 and 11 list requirements for this church office. Since Paul has just specified that he is listing qualifications for the office of deacon with no hint whatsoever that he is now considering a different office and since the next verse continues with other qualifications for deacons, there should be no dispute that these are requirements for women deacons. John Chrysostom confirms this: "He speaks of those having the office of deacon . . . women deacons."[7]

The word for "women" (*gynē*) in verse 11 can refer to either women or wives, depending on the context. Excluding five ambiguous cases, Paul uses *gynē* twenty-eight times meaning "woman" and twenty-eight times meaning "wife." Twenty of the twenty-eight meaning "wife" have an article, "the." Excluding Paul's two chapters about marriage, 1 Corinthians 7 and Ephesians 5, only six clearly mean "wife." In each, the context is husband-wife relations.

The context here, however, is not marriage. No "husbands" or "wives" are mentioned. Nothing limits the reference to wives, such as "their wives" or even an article, "the wives." Furthermore, these are obviously qualifications for an office. Qualifications are appropriate if this regards women deacons but not if this regards wives who hold no church office. Besides, Paul does not list qualifications for the wives of the higher office, overseers (or the husbands of overseers, for that matter). So interpreting "women" to mean "wives of deacons" simply does not fit the context.

The next verse removes any doubt that Paul is still talking about the office of deacon: "Deacons must be . . ." (3:12). Paul continues with qualifications for all deacons: "Married deacons must be devoted to their spouse and take good care of their children and their home." As you might expect, the word referring to marital faithfulness is the same idiom as before, "men of one woman." The fact that "men of one woman" follows qualifications for women deacons that closely parallel the qualifications already stated for deacons makes it clear, as Chrysostom asserted, that "men of one woman" "is appropriate to say regarding women."[8] This idiom follows common convention in using male-oriented terminology to refer to both men and women. Furthermore, 1 Tim. 3:12's "take good care of their children and their home" is particularly appropriate for women. Why didn't Paul list requirements for women overseers? He didn't need to because right after writing about women, "whoever" (*tis*) in 3:1 makes it clear that the requirements are for anyone.

NOTES

1. James Hope Moulton, *An Introduction to the Study of New Testament Greek*, 5th ed., rev. Henry G. Meecham (London: Epworth, 1955), 108–9.

2. BDAG 79, "someone, a person."

3. *Homily 11 on 1 Timothy 3.*

4. G. H. Hugenberger, "Women in Church Office: Hermeneutics or Exegesis? A Survey of Approaches to 1 Timothy 2:8–15," JETS 35/3 (1992): 341–60, at 360 n. 78.

5. Literal translation by this author from *Homily 11 on 1 Timothy 3*: Διάκονοι ἐστωσαν μιᾶς γυναικος ἀνδρες. Ταῦτα και περι γυναικῶν διακόνων ἁρμόττει εἰρῆσθαι. PG 62:545ff and https://greekdownloads3.files.wordpress.com/2014/08/in-epistulam-i-ad-timotheum.pdf.

6. Thomas R. Schreiner, "Philip Payne on Familiar Ground: A Review of Philip B. Payne, *Man and Woman, One in Christ: An Exegetical and Theological Study of Paul's Letters*," *Journal of Biblical Manhood and Womanhood* (Spring 2010), 33–46. Schreiner acknowledges, "The requirements for elders in 1 Tim 3:1–7 and Titus 1:6–9, including the statement that they are to be one-woman men, does not necessarily in and of itself preclude women from serving as elders" (35). Moo admits that "man of one woman" need not exclude "unmarried men or females from the office. . . . It would be going too far to argue that the phrase clearly excludes women." Douglas J. Moo, "The Interpretation of 1 Timothy 2:11–15: A Rejoinder," *TJ* 2 NS (1981): 198–222, at 211. Grudem, *Evangelical Feminism*, 80, correctly argues that "man of one woman" is "not intended to rule out a single man (such as Jesus or Paul) from being an elder." This necessarily entails that "man of one woman" cannot describe *all* elders, which contradicts Grudem's assertion on p. 263 n. 107 that "husband of one wife" is a necessary

qualification for "each" deacon and that it excludes women. Grudem incorrectly adds "each" where there is no such word in the Greek of 1 Tim. 3:12.

7. Homily 11 on 1 Timothy 3, "ἀλλα περι τῶν το ἀξίωμα τῆς διακονίας ἐχουσῶν λέγει . . . γυναικῶν διακόνων."

8. Citation above, p. 153 and n. 5 on p. 157.

Twelve

ELDER REQUIREMENTS AND INSTRUCTIONS

Titus 1–2

WELCOME TO CRETE

Paul and Titus worked together in Crete planting churches (Titus 1:5). Titus was a wonderful, encouraging brother in Christ. He is mentioned many times in 2 Corinthians, including:

> But God, who comforts the downcast, comforted us by the coming of Titus. (2 Cor. 7:6)

> Thanks be to God, who put into the heart of Titus the same concern I have for you. For Titus not only welcomed our appeal, but he is coming to you with much enthusiasm and on his own initiative. (2 Cor. 8:16–17)

Paul eventually left Crete and left Titus to continue the work there.

Paul gives us some insights into the rebellious people Titus faced in Crete. I think the Christian exiles mentioned in 1 Peter (discussed previously) have it worse than the Christians in Crete, but not by much. Just look at how Paul talks about the Cretans:

> For there are many rebellious people, full of meaningless talk and deception, especially those of the circumcision group. They must be silenced, because they are disrupting whole households by teaching things they ought not to teach—and that for the sake of dishonest gain. One of Crete's own prophets has said it: "Cretans are always liars, evil brutes, lazy gluttons." This saying is true. Therefore rebuke them sharply, so that they will be sound in the faith and will pay no attention to Jewish myths or to the merely human commands of those who reject the truth. To the pure, all things are pure, but to those who are corrupted and do not believe, nothing is pure. In fact, both their minds and consciences are corrupted. They claim to know God, but by their actions they deny him. They are detestable, disobedient and unfit for doing anything good. (Titus 1:10–16)

It is because of people who claim to know God but disrupt whole households by teaching things they ought not teach that Titus needs to appoint elders who can correct their deceptions.

ELDER QUALIFICATIONS (TITUS 1:6–9)

The first and main task for Titus was to appoint elders qualified to lead the churches in Crete and address the numerous challenges they faced. Paul lists these qualifications for elders:

> **5** I left you behind on Crete to put in order what is lacking and to appoint elders in every town, as I directed you. **6** Consider anyone who has integrity, is devoted to one spouse

(if married), and whose children believe and are not accused of being wild or disobedient. **7** For the overseer, as a manager of God's household, must have integrity, must not be arrogant, quick-tempered, a heavy drinker or a bully, or pursue dishonest gain, **8** but must be hospitable, one who loves what is good, temperate, upright, holy and disciplined, **9** holding firmly to the trustworthy message as it has been taught, in order to be able to encourage others by sound doctrine and to refute those who oppose it. (Titus 1:5–9)

Paul introduces these requirements for elders with "if anyone" (*ei tis*) in 1:6. *Ei tis* includes women, as it does all fifty-two times in the New Testament (thirty in Paul's letters) when it identifies a person without further specification. So, as it does in 1 Tim. 3:1's introduction to overseer requirements, *tis* includes both men and women. The RSV and NIV add "man" to verse 6, but "man" is not in the Greek text. Paul again uses the phrase "men of one woman" that John Chrysostom wrote "is appropriate to say regarding women."[1] And once again, there are no words such as "he," "him," or "his" or anything that would exclude women. So, as in 1 Timothy 3, all these qualifications are appropriate for women as well as men.

INSTRUCTIONS FOR ELDERS (TITUS 2:1–8)

I must admit that until very recently, I simply assumed that Titus 2:1–8 gave instructions for older men, older women, younger women, and younger men, just like the NIV conveys, but Paul's wording and the context favor the following translation:

1 You, however, must continue to teach sound doctrine.
2 Teach church elders to be temperate, worthy of respect,

self-controlled, and sound in faith, in love and in endurance.
3 Teach the women elders similarly to live as those employed
in sacred service, not to be slanderers or slaves to drink, but
to be teachers of what is excellent, **4** so they can instruct the
younger women in good judgment: to love their husbands and
children, **5** to be self-controlled, pure, good household managers, kind, submitting to their own husbands so that no one will
malign the word of God. **6** Urge the young elders similarly to be
self-controlled **7** in everything, showing yourself to be a model
of good works, in teaching that shows integrity, seriousness
8 and soundness of speech that cannot be condemned, so that
those who oppose you may be ashamed because they have
nothing bad to say about us. (Titus 2:1–8)

CHURCH ELDER OR OLD MAN?

To help you appreciate the discoveries that changed my mind,
I have a question for you. What is an "elder"? Is it a church offi-
cer, or an old person? The answer may be either, depending on
the context. When Paul mentions elders in the previous chapter
(Titus 1:5), he refers to the church office of elder and uses the
Greek word *presbyteros*.[2] But the NIV translates "*older men*" in
Titus 2:2 from a slightly different word, *presbytēs*.[3] You might be
inclined, therefore, to think that there is a simple rule:

presbyteros = church elder
presbytēs = old man

Unfortunately, while that would be a nice simple rule, it is
wrong. It turns out that the Bible uses both words with either
meaning. For example, in 1 Tim. 5:1, Paul tells Timothy not to

rebuke older men, using the same word that in Titus 1:5 means church "elder," *presbyteros*. So *presbyteros* can mean either church "elder" or "old man."

There is one clear case in the New Testament where *presbytēs* means "old man." Luke 1:7 states, *"Elizabeth was not able to conceive, and they were both very old."* When the angel of the Lord announces, *"Your wife Elizabeth will bear you a son"* (1:13), Zechariah replies, *"How can I be sure of this? I am an old man [presbytēs], and my wife is well along in years"* (1:18). Although Zechariah was a priest and so might also have been an elder, Luke clearly refers here to his age.

Presbytēs, however, also refers to anyone with the office of "elder" in the Greek Old Testament at Lam. 4:16, *"The priests are shown no honor, the elders [presbytēs[4]] no favor"*; Num. 10:31, "thou shalt be an elder [*presbytēs*] among us";[5] and Job 29:7–8, which identifies *presbytēs*[6] rising to honor Job. In addition to cases where *presbytai* means "elders," it frequently has the similarly authoritative meaning "ambassador."[7] The *Patristic Greek Lexicon* 1131 lists *presbytēs* as meaning "aged man," a "source of orthodox teaching and apostolic tradition," "an ancient teacher," or "a senior man of authority." Additionally, some Bible versions translate this word in Titus 2:2 "elders" and its feminine form in 2:3 "female elders."[8] So there is ample evidence that *presbytēs* can refer either to someone with the office of "elder" or to an "old man."

Some Greek Bible manuscripts even use the two words *presbyteros* and *presbytēs* interchangeably to mean "elder."[9] In Lamentations 5 they both mean "elder" and are separated by just eleven words: "The elders [*presbyteros*[10]] were not honored" (5:12) and "The elders [*presbytēs*[11]] ceased from the gate" (5:14), where elders would gather to make judgments.

The word for "female elders" (*presbytidas*) in Titus 2:3 is precisely the same form of the same word that the fourth-century

Council of Laodicea canon XI used to forbid the appointment of "female elders." In other documents besides the Bible, *presbytidas* also means "female presbyter" including the *Apocryphal Acts of Matthew* 28 and third-to fourth-century inscriptions to "Angelos Epiktous elder" and "women elders."[12] These examples show that Paul could refer to female elders and that there were female elders early in church history.

SEVEN EVIDENCES THAT TITUS 2:1–8
ADDRESSES CHURCH ELDERS

Since both *presbyteros* and *presbytēs* can mean either "elder" or "old man," we must examine how they are used in each context to determine their meaning. The key question is whether what Paul says in Titus 2:1–8 is more appropriate regarding old people or regarding church elders. The translation "elder" fits this context best and explains the close parallels between these verses and Paul's passages about elders. Titus 2 gives instructions to elders in general and then specific instructions for female elders and young elders like Titus. There are seven reasons that cause me to conclude that the groups of people Paul addresses here are church elders and not simply old or young men or women.

First, the context: after listing the qualifications for elders, Paul describes the urgency of appointing elders in Crete. Here at the start of chapter 2, it makes sense that Paul would now instruct Titus about what he should teach these recently appointed elders. In chapter 3, Paul gives Titus some commands for all the Christians in Crete. But here at the beginning of chapter 2, Paul's focus is on elders.

Second, the introductory command: this passage begins with the command for Titus to "*teach what is appropriate to sound* *doctrine.*" This parallels Paul's earlier stated desire for elders to "*encourage others by sound doctrine and refute those who oppose it*" (1:9, also 1 Tim. 3:2). This focus on teaching sound doctrine is more appropriate for elders than for groups distinguished only by age and sex.

Third, the three-fold structure: Paul instructs Titus what to teach to three groups using the unmistakable structure: "elders . . . women elders similarly . . . young elders similarly." If Paul had intended Titus to convey four messages to four groups of old and young distinguished by sex, one would expect a straightforward listing of the four groups, like Paul gives in 1 Tim. 5:1–2:

> *Do not rebuke an older man harshly, but exhort him as if he were your father. Treat younger men as brothers, older women as mothers, and younger women as sisters, with absolute purity.*

Titus 2:2–8, however, tells Titus what to teach to *three* groups, each set of instructions connected by "similarly" (*hōsautōs*): elders, women elders, and young elders.[13] There is no "similarly" nor any command for Titus to teach the young women. Rather, Titus is to teach the women elders to be teachers of what is excellent so that (*hina*) the younger women will be loving and wise.[14]

Fourth, all the parallels to elder qualifications: all the commands in Titus 2:2–6 closely parallel the qualifications Paul gave for elders in Titus 1:5–9 and 1 Tim. 3:1–7[15] and/or deacons in 1 Tim. 3:8–13:

- He tells the elders in Titus 2:2 to be:
  - **temperate**—*Nēphalios* characterizes overseers (1 Tim. 3:2) and women deacons (1 Tim. 3:11). An elder must not be a "drunkard" (Titus 1:7).

- ○ **worthy of respect—**Semnos· is the first requirement for both deacons and female deacons (1 Tim. 3:8, 11).
- ○ **self-controlled—**Sōphrōn characterizes both elders (Titus 1:8) and overseers (1 Tim. 3:2).
- ○ **sound in faith—**Paul repeats the word for "sound," hugi-ainō, used in the parallel "faith" requirement for elders in Titus 1:9: "*Hold firmly to the trustworthy message as it has been taught*" and parallels the "faith" requirement for deacons in 1 Tim. 3:9.
- ○ **[sound in] love—**This is similar to the requirement that an elder be a "*lover of goodness*" (Titus 1:8) and that an overseer be "*hospitable*" (1 Tim. 3:2).
- ○ **[sound in] endurance—**This is similar both to the "*not . . . a recent convert*" overseer requirement (1 Tim. 3:6) and the "faithful in all things" (1 Tim. 3:11 NRSV) female deacon requirement.

- Similarly, all of Paul's instructions for female elders in Titus 2:3 parallel the requirements for elders in Titus 1, overseers, and/or deacons:
  - ○ **"not . . . slanderers"—**Paul uses the same word, diabolous, twice regarding overseers (1 Tim. 3:6–7), here identical to the requirement for female deacons (1 Tim. 3:11).
  - ○ **not "slaves to drink"—**This applies also to elder, overseer, deacon (Titus 1:7; 1 Tim. 3:2, 3, 8 [with identical mē oinō pollō], 11).
  - ○ **"teachers of what is excellent"—**This instruction is for elders and overseers: "able to give instruction in sound doctrine" (Titus 1:9 RSV); "an apt teacher" (1 Tim. 3:2 NRSV).
- Finally, Paul commands Titus to encourage the young elders like himself to be "*self-controlled*." Sōphrōn characterizes both elders (Titus 1:8) and overseers (1 Tim. 3:2).

All these instructions are especially important for elders, and many of them do not describe all believers. It would be unrealistic to command all older men, especially new believers, to be "sound in faith and endurance" because this takes time and training. Nor are all older women gifted or trained to be "teachers of what is excellent."

Fifth, the ministry term "priestlike": the word that the NIV translates "reverent" (*hieroprepēs*) in Titus 2:3 means "like those employed in sacred service," "priestlike," or suitable for "a sacred . . . person."[16] It combines *hieros*, "pertinent to being of transcendent purity, holy"[17] or "filled with or manifesting divine power,"[18] and *prepō*, "be fitting."[19] All seventy-one times the related word *hieron* occurs in the New Testament, it refers to the temple in Jerusalem (e.g., 1 Cor. 9:13). Behavior befitting the temple fits female elders better than old women.

Sixth, "be teachers of what is excellent": Paul commands Titus to teach women elders to be "teachers of what is excellent [*kalodidaskalous*]" (2:3), a word that Paul apparently coined. It occurs nowhere else in surviving Greek literature, correspondence, or inscriptions. Since teaching is a task assigned to elders (Titus 1:9; 1 Tim. 3:2), it is most appropriate to understand this group as female elders.

Seventh, "model teaching that shows integrity": Paul commands Titus to be a model to other young elders of "good deeds [*kalōn ergōn*], in teaching that shows integrity, seriousness, and sound speech that cannot be condemned" (Titus 2:6–8). In this sentence in Greek, "in teaching" follows immediately after "model of good deeds" and so highlights the particular "good deeds" Paul wants Titus to model. Furthermore, "so that . . . they have nothing *bad* to say" (2:8) is logically related both to its opposite, "*good* deeds" (2:7), and to "teaching that shows integrity." This further links good deeds to teaching. Therefore, Paul calls Titus to be a model to the young elders "in teaching that shows integrity." But why does Titus need to model good teaching? Because Paul wants these young elders to follow Titus's model in teaching that shows integrity. Teaching is a task assigned to elders, so this command fits elders best. The RSV and NRSV conceal this by separating "in your teaching" from "good deeds" by adding "and," but there is no "and" in Greek. The NIV further conceals this by putting "in your teaching" into a separate sentence.

What Paul writes regarding all three groups in Titus 2:2–8, therefore, is more appropriate for elders than for older men and women and younger men. Everything Paul writes about all three groups is appropriate for church elders.

Not only does Paul specifically identify women elders in 2:3, the introduction to the elder requirements, but "if anyone" (ei tis) in Titus 1:6 also includes women. Consequently, both Titus 1:6 and 2:3 affirm female elders.

TITUS 2: ANSWERS TO OBJECTIONS

"The older women are only told to teach by example, not by spoken instruction."

Nothing in the context supports the idea that the teaching here is to be "only" by example. Of course, there are nonverbal aspects to teaching, but every other time Paul uses any word related to "teach" (didaskō), it entails verbal content, and verses 4–5 identify some of that content.

"The older women are told to teach only younger women."

Paul did not write that these women may teach only younger women. Paul gives examples of what female elders teach as "teachers of what is excellent," but he does not restrict their teaching either in scope or audience. Paul's praise for Timothy's grandmother Lois and mother Eunice for teaching him the Holy Scriptures (2 Tim. 1:5; 3:14–15) shows that younger women were not the only group older women should teach and that the scope of their teaching includes Scripture. Proverbs 31:1 states that King Lemuel's mother taught him the following "inspired utterance." Proverbs 31:26 affirms, "*She speaks with wisdom, and faithful instruction is on her tongue.*"

"How can an 'elder' be 'young'?"

Paul commissions Titus to "*appoint elders* [plural] *in every town*" (Titus 1:5). Every qualification regards spiritual maturity. None regards age. It is clear from the responsibilities that Paul assigns to Titus in Crete, including teaching (Titus 1:9; 2:1, 7), and to Timothy in Ephesus (1 Tim. 3:2; 4:6, 11, 13, 16; 5:17; 6:2; 2 Tim. 2:24–25) that they both oversaw churches. Paul tells Timothy, "*Don't let anyone look down on you because you are young*" (1 Tim. 4:12) and calls Titus "*my true son*" (Titus 1:4). How much more, then, could local church overseers be young.

Titus 1:5–9 explains the importance of "Anyone may be an elder who is blameless" by adding in verse 7, "For the overseer, as a manager of God's household, must be blameless." "For" (*gar*) implies a reason or explanation for the preceding elder requirements and so naturally refers to elders. Consequently, "elder" and "overseer" appear to be equivalent. It would be odd for Paul to stress the importance of appointing elders and then give separate lists of requirements for elders and overseers, especially joined by "for." Furthermore, the qualifications for overseers in 1 Tim. 3:2–7 closely parallel those for elders and overseers in Titus 2:2–5.

It is doubtful that all the small house churches Titus oversaw in Crete had multiple mature believers from age fifty to fifty-six, which is how Hippocrates defined "elders."[20] Since Titus was not an "elder" as regards age but had the oversight function of an elder, it is only natural that some of the elders he appointed for these small churches would also be young.

"But young women are told to be subject to their husbands."

These female elders should "instruct the younger women in good judgment: to love their husbands and children, to be self-controlled, pure, good household managers, kind, submitting to their own husbands so that no one will malign the word of God." (Titus 2:4–5)

"Instruct the younger women . . . to love their husbands" shows that just as husbands should love their wives, wives should also love their husbands. This proves that it is false to assume that Paul's commands "to submit" and "to love" in Ephesians 5 apply, respectively, only to wives and only to husbands. Ephesians 5 commands wives to submit in the context of "submitting to one another."

Widows and women dedicated to celibate service for Christ (1 Cor. 7:25–38) do not have husbands, so the husband-related instructions here should not be interpreted as commands for all women.

Most of these qualities are reminiscent of the noble wife in Proverbs 31:10–31, and all of them describe "good wives" in Paul's day. Paul gives a specific reason why younger women should submit to their husbands, and it is not because God has delegated husbands to have authority over their wives. It is "*so that no one will malign the word of God.*" That's right. Paul wants younger women to adhere to cultural norms so that others will speak well of the gospel. Greek literature confirms that wives in that culture were expected to do each of the things Paul lists here. Because unsubmissive wives undermined conventional norms, they could lead people to reject the gospel. Similarly, a few verses later Titus 2:9–10 calls *"slaves to be subject to their masters in everything . . . so that in every way they will make the teaching about God our Savior attractive."* By being submissive according to cultural norms, both wives and slaves made the gospel more attractive, especially to their husbands and masters. We also saw this idea in the earlier section about 1 Peter. This evangelistic incentive flows from the more theological incentive: to imitate Christ by subordinating our interests to love and serve others.

NOTES

1. Citation above, pp. 153 and 157 n. 5.
2. Paul here uses *presbyterous*, the accusative form of the word *presbyteros*.
3. Paul here uses *presbytas*, the accusative form of *presbytēs*.
4. In its direct-object plural form, *presbytas*.
5. Translation from *The Septuagint Version of the Old Testament with an English Translation* (Grand Rapids: Zondervan, 1970), 979.
6. In its plural form, *presbytai*.
7. In LXX 2 Chron. 32:31; 1 Macc. 14:21, 22; 15:17; 2 Macc. 11:34, as does *presbys* in Num. 21:21; 22:5; Deut. 2:26; Isa. 57:9. LSJ 1462 says *presbeutēs* (a variant spelling of *presbytēs*) means "ambassador." The RSV, RSVCE, TEV, NEB, REB, MSG, and BDAG 861, 863 translate *presbytēs* as "ambassador" in Philem. 9.
8. The Passion Translation: Titus 2:2 "male elders," Titus 2:3 "female elders." The Orthodox Jewish Bible translates *presbytas* in Titus 2:2 "Zekenim," *presbytidas* in Titus 2:3 "the senior women, the Zekanot," and *presbytēs* in Philemon 9 "the Zaken (Elder)." Aída Besançon Spencer also argues that Titus 2:2–3 is about elders and female elders in "Leadership of Women in Crete and Macedonia as a Model for the Church," *Priscilla Papers* 27, 4 (Autumn 2013): 5–15; and in *2 Timothy and Titus*, New Covenant Commentary Series (Eugene, OR: Wipf & Stock, 2014).
9. These two words, *presbyteros* and *presbytēs*, occur interchangeably in Codex Vaticanus's text of Susanna (Dan. 13 in the LXX) to describe "two elders of the people [who] were appointed judges" (Sus. 5 NAB). These words are so interchangeable that in seven instances Codex Vaticanus and Theodotion's

translation have presbytai where Codex Alexandrinus and Codex Marchalianus (Q) have presbytēroi, all meaning "elders." In Susanna 18–19, presbytēroi is separated from "the two presbytai" by only eleven words in Vaticanus.

10. In its plural form, presbytēroi.

11. In its plural form, presbytai.

12. IGC As. Min., 167 cited in PGL 1131. These inscriptions have presbytidos and gynaikōn presbytidōn. Bernadette J. Brooten, *Inscriptional Evidence for Women Leaders in the Ancient Synagogue: Inscriptional Evidence and Background Issues*, BJS 36 (Atlanta: Scholars Press, 1982), 41–46, cites six inscriptions identifying women elders including "Here lies Sara Ura, elder."

13. Hōsautōs is the same word Paul uses in a similar context in 1 Tim. 3:8 and 11 to indicate that deacons and female deacons, like overseers, have necessary qualifications. Hōsautōs implies a similarity that is more appropriate to link instructions specifically for elders than to link instructions for unrelated groups distinguished only by age and sex.

14. "Similarly" is not repeated regarding slaves in Titus 2:9–10. Titus 1:10's "there are many insubordinate men" shows that Paul was aware of issues in the churches in Crete that probably motivated these strong words to slaves.

15. Elders = overseers in Titus 1:5, 7; Acts 20:17, 28, "the elders of the church . . . in which the Holy Spirit has made you overseers"; and 1 Pet. 5:1–5, "elders . . . episkopountes . . . elders."

16. LSJ 822.

17. BDAG 470.

18. LSJ 822.

19. BDAG 861.

20. Philo, Op. Mundi 105, writes: "Solon, then, reckons the life of man by the aforesaid ten weeks of years [namely seventy years, with presbytou followed only by gerontos]. And Hippocrates the physician, says that 'There are seven ages, those of the little boy, the boy, the lad, the young man, the man, the elderly man, the old man, and that these ages are measured by multiples of seven . . . a man till forty-nine, till seven times seven; an elderly man [presbytēs] till fifty-six, up to seven times eight; after that an old man [gerōn].'" LCL Philo 1:84–87.

CONCLUSION

Ten Biblical Principles that
Entail Gender Equality

We have considered all the relevant Bible passages. In summary, we have learned that men and women should live, work, and serve with each other as equals. From these passages we can draw ten important principles that will guide us in how we apply the biblical truth that men and women share equal rights and responsibilities.

1. MALE AND FEMALE ARE EQUALLY
CREATED IN GOD'S IMAGE

Genesis teaches and Paul reiterates that all people are created in God's image. Their new nature is *"being renewed in knowledge in the image of its Creator"* (Col. 3:10; cf. 2 Cor. 3:18). Paul argues that men and women should both respect each other as their source, for *"just as woman came from man, so also man comes through woman"* (1 Cor. 11:12).[1]

Since humanity as male and female is in God's image, God cannot be exclusively male. Indeed, God as Spirit cannot be male at all. Accordingly, Paul's reflections on the human Jesus always use the inclusive word *anthrōpos* ("human," e.g., Phil. 2:7; 1 Tim. 2:5).[2] This word occurs in the phrase that is typically translated "the Son of Man" (*ho huios tou anthrōpou*). Since, however, *anthrōpou* means "human" with no male nuance, and because Jesus did not have a human father, it should be translated "the human Son." "Son" is the primary subject (nominative) that is modified by "human" (genitive), so it expresses the divine Son who is human. Jesus usually used "the human Son" to describe himself in contexts that highlight his authority[3] or his suffering, death, and resurrection.[4] This is why when Jesus asks, "Who do people say that the human Son is?" Peter answers, "You are the Christ, the Son of the living God" (Matt. 16:13–16). Only as truly human could the Son "*give his life as a ransom for many*" (Matt. 20:28; Mark 10:45).

2. MALE AND FEMALE EQUALLY RECEIVED THE CREATION MANDATE AND BLESSING

Paul reflects the creation mandate and blessing given to humanity as male and female (Gen. 1:26–30) in his affirmation in 1 Tim. 6:17, "Put [your] *hope in God, who richly provides us with everything for our enjoyment.*" Similarly, Paul's repeated affirmations of freedom and of food as gifts from God and his rejection of dietary restrictions (e.g., 1 Cor. 10:23–30), each without gender distinction, are based on woman's, as well as man's, authority over all other earthly creatures.

3. REDEEMED MEN AND WOMEN ARE EQUALLY "IN CHRIST"

The ultimate identity marker in Paul's theology is being "in Christ." Those who are "in Christ" are part of Christ's body.

Believers who are "in Christ" are thereby righteous and at peace with God. At the heart of Paul's theology is the unity of all who are redeemed "in Christ." There is no requirement for salvation that distinguishes men from women.[5] "Everyone who calls on the name of the Lord will be saved" (Rom. 10:13). In our standing in Christ, too, it makes no difference whatsoever whether we are male or female (Gal. 3:28). Specifically in the context of worship leadership in both prayer and prophecy, Paul affirms, literally, "woman is not separate from man nor is man separate from woman in the Lord" (1 Cor. 11:11).[6]

4. CHURCH LEADERSHIP AS SERVICE

The nature of Christian leadership and authority entails humble service, following Christ's example (Matt. 20:25–28; Luke 22:25–27; John 13:1–17; Phil. 2:7).[7] Christian leadership is based on love, willingness to serve, and spiritual gifts, not on wisdom, strength, or influence as the world sees these (1 Cor. 1–2). Indeed, "deacon" (*diakonos*) means "servant," and "servant" and "slave" (*doulos*) are two of Paul's favorite self-designations.[8] When Paul refers to others as a "servant" or "slave" of Christ, it is high praise indeed.[9]

The only person the New Testament identifies by name as an "overseer" is Christ, and no one as a local church "elder." John refers to himself as "the elder" in 2 John 1 and 3 John 1, and Peter refers to himself as "a fellow elder, a witness of Christ's sufferings" in 1 Pet. 5:1, but these do not refer to a local church office, but rather to their apostolic role as eyewitnesses of Jesus. The only person the New Testament names as having a local church office is "Phoebe, deacon of the church in Cenchreae." The New Testament depicts church leadership by a group of overseers (Phil. 1:1; Titus 1:7).[10] Furthermore, authority in the church is anchored in God's Word, not in ministers per se—not even Paul: "*But even if we or an angel from heaven should preach a gospel other than the one we preached to you, let them be under God's curse!*" (Gal. 1:8). Similarly, prophets should "*weigh [prophecies] carefully*" (1 Cor. 14:29) to ensure conformity with the apostolic message and the Scriptures.

Consequently, church leaders' authority is not intrinsic to themselves or their office but is derived. Their authority is inextricably tied to the work of the Holy Spirit, who gives the necessary gifts for leadership and who guides the leader (Acts 20:28). They exercise this authority by faithfully expounding Scripture. Their words have no authority if they go against Scripture (Acts 17:11), and their deeds are subject to Scripture. The way Paul describes his female colleagues shows that he believed the Spirit not only gifts women as well as men for church leadership, but guides them into ministry as well.

5. MUTUAL SUBMISSION IN THE CHURCH AND HOME

"Submitting to one another out of reverence for Christ" is a natural outgrowth of being "*filled with the Spirit*" (Eph. 5:18–21; cf. 1 John 4:13, 16). Mutual submission is reflected in and related to Paul's "one another" statements such as Gal. 5:13, "*Serve one another humbly in love*"; Rom. 12:10, "*Honor one another above yourselves*"; and Eph. 4:2, "*Be completely humble and gentle; be patient, bearing with one another in love.*" Paul does not limit any of these to only one gender. If only one party submits, it is not mutual. Ephesians 5:21's reciprocal pronoun requires that mutual submission goes both ways. It means that each person treats the other as more important than themselves. It undergirds the nature of Christian leadership as humble service.

Ephesians 5:22 applies Paul's general command in 5:21 for believers to submit to one another specifically to the relationship between husband and wife. Paul's following explanation of mutual husband-wife obligations bears this out, particularly as he explains his "head" metaphor.[11] Paul gives Christ's self-sacrifice as a model for husbands (and all believers, Eph. 5:2) to love, nourish, and care for their wives. Colossians 3:18–19, a close parallel to Eph. 5:21–22, should be understood in the context of verses 12–17's demand for "*compassion, kindness, humility, gentleness and patience. Bear with each other and forgive one another. . . . Teach and admonish one another.*"

In 1 Cor. 7:1–16, Paul expresses the rights and responsibilities of husbands and wives with exactly parallel terminology regarding eleven issues.[12] Verse 4 even states, "The husband does not have authority over his own body, but his wife does." Verse 5 requires "harmonious agreement." Verses 14 and 16 affirm mutuality in spiritual relations. Paul also affirms woman's capacity for leadership in the home in 1 Tim. 5:14 by calling younger women to marry and "*to manage their homes*" (*oikodespotein*), which combines the word meaning "house" with the word from which "despot" comes.

Alongside Paul's teaching on mutual submission, he calls wives to submit to their husbands, children to obey their parents, and slaves to obey their masters. Comparison with secular "house tables" shows that Paul gives these conventions a decidedly egalitarian twist.[13] Following Christ's model, the husband should give himself in love for his wife. This gives his wife security and kindles her respect (Eph. 5:33) and love (Titus 2:4). As husband and wife mutually submit to the other's desires, they experience a deeper and deeper unity (Eph. 5:28, 30, 31)—not the unity of ruler and subordinate, but of coequals, each free to take initiative, neither with the final say. The husband's self-giving love and the wife's submission cause the relationship to flourish. Eph. 5:21–33 is thus a grand charter for a marriage relationship modeled after Christ's love and self-giving.

Similarly, Peter gives a series of imperatives to submit in 1 Pet. 2:13, 18; 3:1, 7. *"Wives, in the same way* [homoiōs] *submit your-selves to your own husbands"* in 3:1 pairs with 3:7, "Husbands, in the same way [homoiōs] submit to your own wives,[14] dwelling together wisely, recognizing her as a weaker feminine precious vessel, and assign them the honor they deserve as coheirs with you of the gracious gift of life, so that your prayers won't be hindered."

6. THE ONENESS OF THE BODY OF CHRIST

The church is the "body of Christ." Paul insists in 1 Cor. 12:25 *"that there should be no division in the body, but that its parts should have equal concern for each other."* Since Paul explains that different parts of the body have different functions, it is clear he does not advocate that all believers are the same or all do the same thing. Rather, the division he opposes is for one part to put itself over other parts—namely, through competitive ranking. Stratification of status is antithetical to the oneness of the body. Furthermore, according to Eph. 4:12, all members—women and men—should minister to and build up the body of Christ.

7. THE PRIESTHOOD OF ALL BELIEVERS

1 Peter 2:5 and 9 affirm the priesthood of all believers. In 2 Cor. 3:12–18, Paul implies the universal priesthood of believers. Colossians 3:16 expresses his desire that all Christians, women as well as men, will have a teaching ministry: *"Let the message of Christ*

dwell among you richly as you teach and admonish one another with all wisdom." Similarly, 1 Cor. 14:26 affirms, "When you assemble, each one has . . . a word of instruction [literally, 'a teaching']." The priesthood of all believers is incompatible with excluding women from the priesthood. Indeed, it presupposes the equal standing and priestly responsibilities of men and women.

8. THE SPIRIT GIFTS ALL BELIEVERS

For Paul, church worship and the structure of church authority are intimately connected with the gifts of the Spirit. He states, "To each one the manifestation of the Spirit is given for the common good" (1 Cor. 12:7; cf. Rom. 12:6–8), and in 1 Cor. 12:11, "the same Spirit . . . distributes them to each one, just as he determines." Thus, all women, just as all men, have spiritual gifts and are responsible to use them not in seclusion but "for the common good." Indeed, in 1 Cor. 12:31 and 14:1, Paul urges all believers, women as well as men, "Eagerly desire the greater gifts [i.e., to be apostles, prophets, teachers] . . . especially prophecy." Excluding women from such forms of ministry doesn't simply deprive the church; it disobeys God's command.

Following the Old Testament tradition of women prophets such as Miriam, Huldah, and Deborah, and New Testament prophets such as Anna and the four daughters of Philip, Paul permitted women to prophesy. He states clearly in 1 Cor. 14:31, "You can all prophesy" (cf. 11:5; 14:5, 24, 26, 39). In announcing the advent of the age of the Spirit, Peter declares, "Your . . . daughters will prophesy. . . . Even on my servants, both men and women, I will pour out my Spirit in those days, and they will prophesy" (Acts 2:17–18). Believers should recognize gifts in women in exactly the same way they do in men, by testing the gift in practical ministry and seeing whether or not the Spirit blesses. Who dares oppose the Spirit's gifting and guiding women into ministry?

9. LIBERTY IN CHRIST

Paul, the "Apostle of Liberty," never distinguished the freedom of men from that of women. Shortly after his statement "there is no male-female division, *for you are all one in Christ Jesus*" (Gal. 3:28), he writes, "*It is for freedom that Christ has set us free. Stand firm, then, and do not let yourselves be burdened again by a yoke of slavery*" (5:1). This is addressed to all the congregations in Galatia and cannot be restricted to men alone. For Paul, arbitrarily stratified status is repugnant, whether determined by race, nationality, economics, or gender.

Paul himself was remarkably free from the restraints of male stereotypes. In 1 Thess. 2:7, he depicts himself caring for the Thessalonians with the tender affection of a nursing mother holding her child to her breast,[15] and in Gal. 4:19 he describes himself as "*in the pains of childbirth*." He was no chauvinist who needed to protect a fragile male ego. His identity was secure in Christ. In applying to himself female imagery, Paul followed the example of Jesus, who said, "*How often I have longed to gather your children together, as a hen gathers her chicks under her wings*" (Matt. 23:37; Luke 13:34). Jesus identifies with the plight of the daughters of Jerusalem even on the road to his crucifixion (Luke 23:27–31).

10. IN CHRIST, MALE AND FEMALE ARE EQUAL

"There is no Jew-Greek division, there is no slave-free division, there is no male-female division, for you are all one in Christ

Jesus" (Gal. 3:28) repudiates divisions and declares that all in the body of Christ have equal worth and equal inheritance of the salvation promises.[16] James 2:1–13 similarly prohibits favoritism based on wealth. In Christ, these groups do not stand on different levels but are equals. Galatians 3:28 is not concerned only with who can be saved. Paul did everything he could to apply the implications of Gal. 3:28 to the social dimensions of the church, even rebuking Peter for withdrawing from table fellowship with gentiles (Gal. 2:11–14). The high proportion of women in Paul's circle of ministry and the many gentiles, slaves, and women in his churches show that Paul would oppose the idea that gentiles, slaves, and women can be saved but may not hold offices of leadership in the church. Galatians 3:28 does not deny sexual differences, but it does repudiate any second-class status or exclusion of women from ministries for Christ.

Similarly, 1 Cor. 11:11–12 affirms specifically regarding men and women leading worship in prayer and prophecy: "Neither is woman separate from man, nor is man separate from woman in the Lord."[17] This repudiates any separate treatment or status for women from men, such as excluding women from teaching or leadership positions in the church.

SUMMARY

The biblical theology of man and woman, particularly as articulated by Paul, is based on these ten fundamental principles. Each establishes the equality of men and women: creation in God's image, the creation mandate and blessing, being in Christ, servant leadership, mutual submission in both marriage and church life, the oneness of the body of Christ, the priesthood of all believers, the gifts of the Spirit, liberty in Christ, and equal status in Christ.

These principles provide the theological context for understanding what the Bible teaches about women.

These fundamental biblical principles confirm our thesis that the Bible does not teach "biblical womanhood" understood as male headship (a word that is not in the Bible) and female subordination, as I mistakenly used to believe. There is simply no clear teaching of this anywhere in the Bible. Rather, the Bible teaches mutual submission (Eph. 5:21), that there is "no male-female division in Christ" (Gal. 3:28) and that "woman is not separate from man, nor is man separate from woman in the Lord" (1 Cor. 11:11), specifically regarding leadership in worship.

I hope this book has helped you understand the Bible's teachings on men and women. I came to the Bible desiring to listen to what the Spirit says about men and women and to do my best to understand God's Word as originally written. The Bible transformed my understanding. I trust that you have been listening to what the Bible says about how God desires men and women to serve and lead alongside each other within the church and family, as equals, in whatever ways they are gifted. This has always been God's plan for thriving marriages and Christ-honoring churches.

If you want to go deeper, I recommend the fuller analysis of these passages in my 511-page *Man and Woman, One in Christ: An Exegetical and Theological Study of Paul's Letters* (www.pbpayne.com) or some of the books and articles on this topic by other authors mentioned in the introduction.

NOTES

1. Cf. above, pp. 70–71.
2. *Anēr* ("man/male") in Eph. 4:13, "mature manhood" (RSV), specifically refers to *all* believers, female as well as male, and so is translated "become mature" in the NRSV and NIV.

3. E.g., Matt. 9:6; 12:8; 13:41; 16:27; 19:28; 26:63–64; Mark 14:61–62; Luke 22:69–70.

4. E.g., Matt. 12:40; 17:9, 12, 22–23; 20:18–19, 28; 26:2, 24, 45.

5. Cf. above, pp. 148–49.

6. Cf. above, pp. 69–72.

7. Cf. Efrain Agosto, *Servant Leadership: Jesus and Paul* (St. Louis: Chalice, 2005).

8. Paul calls himself "servant" (*diakonos*) in 1 Cor. 3:5; 2 Cor. 3:6; 6:4; 11:23; Eph. 3:7; Col. 1:23, 25; and "slave" (*doulos*) in Rom. 1:1; 1 Cor. 9:19; 2 Cor. 4:5; Gal. 1:10; Phil. 1:1; Titus 1:1.

9. *Diakonos*: Eph. 6:21; Col. 1:7; 4:7; 1 Thess. 3:2 (most manuscripts); 1 Tim. 4:6. *Doulos* or *syndoulos* ("fellow slave"): Col. 1:7; 4:7, 12; 2 Tim. 2:24.

10. Cf. above, pp. 35, 136, 160, 165, 169–70, 172 n. 15.

11. Cf. above, pp. 111–16, and regarding 1 Cor. 11:3, pp. 51–58.

12. Cf. above, pp. 39–42.

13. Cf. above, p. 113.

14. Cf. above, pp. 128–33.

15. See "nurse" in James Hope Moulton and George Milligan, *The Vocabulary of The Greek New Testament: Illustrated from the Papyri and Other Non-Literary Sources* (London: Hodder & Stoughton, 1930), 643.

16. Cf. above, pp. 103–10.

17. Cf. above, pp. 69–72.

APPENDIX 1

The Sixteen Vaticanus
Distigme-Obelos Symbols

Triangle = insertion point. Four distigmai are on the right side of the open codex's sixth column.

Matthew 6:13 1241B

The distigme matches Vaticanus's original apricot color ink.

Matthew 7:21 1243

The left portion of the obelos matches Vaticanus's original apricot color ink.

Matthew 8:13 1243C

Matthew 13:51 1253B

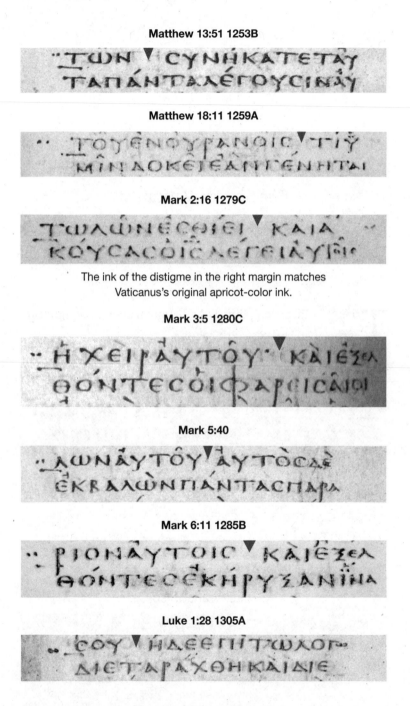

Matthew 18:11 1259A

Mark 2:16 1279C

The ink of the distigme in the right margin matches
Vaticanus's original apricot-color ink.

Mark 3:5 1280C

Mark 5:40

Mark 6:11 1285B

Luke 1:28 1305A

Luke 14:24 1332C

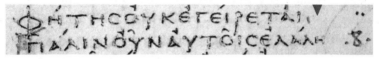

The distigme matches Vaticanus's original apricot color ink.

John 7:53–8:11 1361C

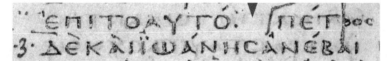

John 14:1 1371C

Acts 2:47 1385B

Acts 6:10 1390

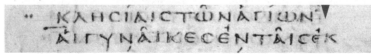

Note the downward dipping ink from both dots and
the bar, indicating a different hand that added it after
Vaticanus was written, and so could not add a gap.

1 Corinthians 14:34–35 1474A

APPENDIX 2

Obelos vs. Paragraph Bar Extension
into the Margin and Length

mm	2.7	2.8	2.9	3.0	3.1	3.2	3.3	3.4	3.5	3.6	3.7	3.8
3.3												
3.2												
3.1												
3.0												
2.9												
2.8												
2.7												
2.6												O
2.5												
2.4												
2.3												¶
2.2										¶		
2.1												
2.0								¶			¶	
1.9	¶											
1.8								¶		¶		
1.7						¶						¶
1.6								¶				
1.5								¶			¶	
1.4												
1.3									¶			
1.2												
1.1								¶				
1.0												
0.9												
0.8								¶				
0.7				¶		¶						
0.6												
0.5								¶				
0.4												
0.3												¶

O = obelos (bar) portion of distigme-obelos symbols   ¶ = paragraph bars by distigme lines

Contrasting Extension into the Margin (vertical axis) and Length (horizontal axis) in mm. of Vaticanus Obeloi (O) in Distigme-Obelos Symbols and Paragraph Bars (¶) by Distigme Lines

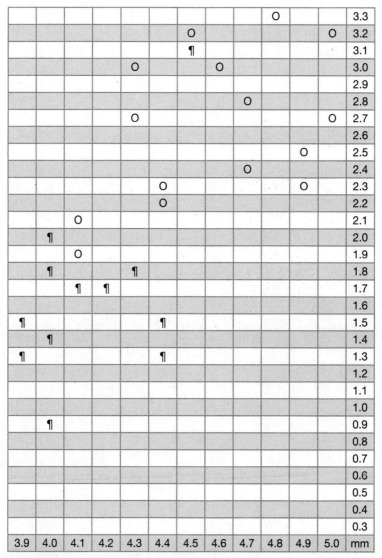

3.9	4.0	4.1	4.2	4.3	4.4	4.5	4.6	4.7	4.8	4.9	5.0	mm
									O			3.3
						O					O	3.2
						¶						3.1
				O			O					3.0
												2.9
								O				2.8
				O						O		2.7
												2.6
									O			2.5
								O				2.4
					O					O		2.3
					O							2.2
		O										2.1
	¶											2.0
	O											1.9
	¶			¶								1.8
		¶	¶									1.7
												1.6
¶					¶							1.5
	¶											1.4
¶					¶							1.3
												1.2
												1.1
												1.0
	¶											0.9
												0.8
												0.7
												0.6
												0.5
												0.4
												0.3

O = obelos (bar) portion of distigme-obelos symbols   ¶ = paragraph bars by distigme lines

SCRIPTURE INDEX

SUBJECT INDEX

AUTHOR INDEX

BIBLIOGRAPHY

Agosto, Efrain. *Servant Leadership: Jesus and Paul.* St. Louis: Chalice, 2005.

Aland, Barbara, Kurt Aland, Johannes Karavidopoulos, Carlo M. [Cardinal] Martini, and Bruce M. Metzger, eds. *The Greek New Testament.* 5th rev. ed.; Stuttgart: Deutsche Bibelgesellschaft, 2014.

Alford, Henry. *The Greek Testament: a Critical and Exegetical Commentary.* 4 vols. London: Rivingtons, 1880.

Andrist, Patrick, ed. *Le manuscrit B de la Bible (Vaticanus graecus 1209) Introduction au fac-similé, Actes du Colloque de Genève (11 juin 2001), Contributions supplémentaires.* Lausanne, Switzerland: Éditions du Zèbre, 2009.

Aubert, J. *Cyrilli Opera.* Paris: Magna Navis, 1638.

Bailly, A. [M. Anatole]. *Dictionnaire Grec Français Rédigé avec le concours de. E. Egger: Édition revue par L. Séchan et. P. Chantraine.* Paris: Librairie Hachette, 1950.

Banks, Robert. *Etymological Dictionary of Greek.* 2 vols.; Leiden/Boston: Brill, 2016.

Barber, E. A. with assistance of P. Mass, M. Scheller and M. L. West, *H. G. Liddell, Robert Scott, H. Stuart Jones Greek-English Lexicon: A Supplement.* Oxford: Clarendon Press, 1968.

Barr, Beth Allison. *The Making of Biblical Womanhood: How the Subjugation of Women Became Gospel Truth.* Grand Rapids: Baker, 2021.

Barrett, C. K. *The Epistle to the Romans.* London: A. & C. Black, 1957.

Bartlett, Andrew. *Men and Women in Christ: Fresh Light from the Biblical Texts.* London: Inter-Varsity, 2019.

BasisBibel. Stuttgart: Deutsche Bibelgesellschaft, 2021.

Bauer, Walter, Frederick W. Danker, W. F. Arndt, F. W. Gingrich, eds. *A Greek-English Lexicon of the New Testament and Other Early Christian Literature.* 3rd edition. Chicago: University of Chicago, 2000. (BDAG)

Bedale, Stephan. "The Meaning of κεφαλή in the Pauline Epistles." *Journal of Theological Studies* 5 n.s. (1954) 211–215.

Beyer, Elizabeth, ed. *Mutual by Design: A Better Model for Christian Marriage.* Minneapolis: CBE International, 2017.

Bölting, Rudolf. *Dicionário Grego-Português.* Rio De Janeiro: Imprensa National, 1941.

Brooten, Bernadette J. *Inscriptional Evidence for Women Leaders in the Ancient Synagogue: Inscriptional Evidence and Background Issues.* BJS 36. Atlanta: Scholars Press, 1982.

Brown, Colin, ed. *The New International Dictionary of New Testament Theology.* 3 vols. Exeter: Paternoster, 1976–1978. (*NIDNTT*)

Brown, Francis, S. R. Driver, and Charles A. Briggs, *A Hebrew and English Lexicon of the Old Testament.* Oxford: Clarendon, 1906. (BDB)

Budé, Guillaume, Jacobus Tusanus, Konrad Gesner, Hadrianus Junius. *Dictionarium Graecolatinum.* Basil: Henri C. Petrina, 1577.

Cervin, Richard S. "Does Κεφαλή [Kephalē] Mean 'Source' or 'Authority Over' in Greek Literature? A Rebuttal." *Trinity Journal* 10 NS (1989) 85–112.

Chantraine, Pierre. *Dictionnaire étymologique de la Langue Grecque: Histoire des Mots.* 4 vols. Paris: Klincksieck, 1968–1980.

Charlesworth, James Hamilton, ed. *The Old Testament Pseudepigrapha.* 2 vols. London: Darton, Longman Todd, 1985. (OTP)

Chicago Statement on Biblical Inerrancy. https://www.etsjets.org/files/documents/Chicago_Statement.pdf.

Colson, F. H., translator. *Philo.* Vols. 6–10 of 10 vols. Loeb Classical Library. Cambridge, MA.: Harvard University Press. Vol. 6: 1935, 7: 1937, 8: 1979, 9: 1979, 10: 1962, 11: 1977.

Colson, F. H. and G. H. Whitaker, translators. *Philo.* Vols. 1–5 of 10 vols. Loeb Classical Library. Cambridge, MA: Harvard University Press. Vol. 1: 1929/1981, 2: 1929, 3: 1930, 4: 1932/1979; 5: 1934.

Cranfield, C. E. B. *A Critical and Exegetical Commentary on the Epistle to the Romans.* ICC. Edinburgh: T&T Clark, 1979.

Danvers Statement. https://cbmw.org/about/danvers-statement/.

Davids, Peter H. "A Silent Witness in Marriage." Pages 224–238 in Ronald W. Pierce and Rebecca Merrill Groothuis, *Discovering Biblical Equality: Complementarity Without Hierarchy.* Downers Grove, IL: InterVarsity Press, 2004.

Duncan, George S. *The Epistle of Paul to the Galatians.* London: Hodder and Stoughton, 1934.

Epp, Eldon Jay. *Junia: The First Woman Apostle.* Minneapolis: Fortress, 2005.

Estienne, Henri. *Thesaurus graecae Linguae.* 8 vols. Geneva: Henr. Stephani Oliva, 1572. Reprinted Paris: A. F. Didot, 1831–1865.

Fee, Gordon D. *The First Epistle to the Corinthians.* NICNT. Grand Rapids: Eerdmans, 1987, rev. ed. 2014.

Feyerabend, K. *Greek-English Dictionary.* New York: Saphrograph, 1971.

Fitzmyer, Joseph A. "Another Look at ΚΕΦΑΛΗ in 1 Corinthians 11.3." *New Testament Studies* 35 (1989) 503–511

_____. First Corinthians: A New Translation with Introduction and Commentary. AB. New Haven: Yale University Press, 2008.

_____. "Kephalē in I Corinthians 11:3." Interpretation 47, 1 (January, 1993) 52–59.

France, R. T. and David Wenham, eds. Gospel Perspectives: Studies of History and Tradition in the Four Gospels. Sheffield: JSOT, 1980.

_____. Gospel Perspectives II. Sheffield: JSOT, 1981.

Friberg, Barbara and Timothy, Analytical Greek New Testament. Grand Rapids: Baker, 1981.

Giles, Kevin. "The Genesis of Confusion: How 'Complementarians' Have Corrupted Communication." Priscilla Papers 29, 1 (2015) 22–29.

_____. Jesus and the Father: Modern Evangelicals Reinvent the Doctrine of the Trinity. Grand Rapids: Zondervan: 2006.

Glare, P. G. W. with the assistance of A. A. Thompson, eds. H. G. Liddell, Robert Scott, H. Stuart Jones, Roderick McKenzie Greek-English Lexicon Revised Supplement. Oxford: Clarendon, 1996.

Grudem, Wayne. Evangelical Feminism & Biblical Truth. Sisters, OR: Multnomah, 2004.

_____. "The Meaning of κεφαλή ('Head') An Evaluation of New Evidence, Real and Alleged." Appendix 4, pages 552–599 in Evangelical Feminism & Biblical Truth: An Analysis of More Than One Hundred Disputed Questions. Sisters, OR: Multnomah, 2004.

Haines-Eitzen, K. The Gendered Palimpsest: Women, Writing, and Representation in Early Christianity. Oxford: Oxford University Press, 2012.

Hallpike, C. R. "Social Hair," Man n.s. 4 (1969) 256–264.

Hart, David Bentley. The New Testament: A Translation. New Haven/London: Yale, 2017.

Herter, H. "Effeminatus." Pages 620–650 in vol. 2 (1954) of Reallexikon für Antike und Christentum: Schwörterbuch zur Ausienandersetzung des Christentums mit der Antiken Welt. 31 vols. Stuttgart: Anton Hiersemann, 1950–2021. (RAC)

Hugenberger, Gordon P. "Women in Church Office: Hermeneutics or Exegesis? A Survey of Approaches to 1 Tim 2:8–15." Journal of the Evangelical Theological Society 35, 3 (September 1992) 341–360.

James, M. R. The Testament of Abraham, the Greek Text now first edited with an Introduction and Notes. Cambridge: Cambridge University Press, 1892.

Jantsch, Torsten. "Die Frau soll Kontrolle über ihren Kopf ausüben (1Kor 11,10). Zum historischen, kulturellen und religi.sen Hintergrund von 1Kor 11,2–16." Pages 97–144 in Frauen, Männer, Engel: Perspektiven zu 1Kor 11,2–16. Ed. Torsten Jantsch. Biblisch-Theologische Studien 152. Neukirchen-Vluyn: Neukirchener Verlag, 2015.

Jenkins, Claude. "Documents: Origen on 1 Corinthians." Journal of Theological Studies 10 (1909) 29–51.

John Paul II, Pope. On the Dignity and Vocation of Women: Mulieris Dignitatem. Boston: Daughters of St. Paul, 1988.

Jongkind, Dirk et al., eds. *The Greek New Testament: Tyndale House, Cambridge.* Cambridge/ Wheaton, IL: Cambridge University Press/Crossway, 2017.

Kelly, J. N. D., *Epistles of Peter & Jude.* New York: Harper and Row and London: Adam & Charles Black, 1969.

Kittel, Gerhard and Gerhard Freidrich, eds. *Theological Dictionary of the New Testament.* Translated and edited by Geoffrey W. Bromiley. 10 vols. Grand Rapids: Eerdmans, 1964–1976. (*TDNT*)

Knight, George W. III. "Husbands and Wives as Analogues of Christ and the Church: Ephesians 5:21–33 and Colossians 3:18–19." Pages 165–178 in *Recovering Biblical Manhood and Womanhood: A Response to Evangelical Feminism.* Edited by John Piper and Wayne Grudem. Wheaton, IL: Crossway, 1991.

_____. "Male and Female Related He Them." *Christianity Today* 20, no. 14 (April 9, 1976) 13–17.

Köhler, Ludwig and Walter Baumgartner. *The Hebrew and Aramaic Lexicon of the Old Testament.* 5 vols. Revised and edited by Walter Baumgartner and Johann Jakob Stamm. Translated and edited under the supervision of M. E. J. Richardson. Leiden: Brill, 1994–2000. (*HALOT*)

Kroeger, Catherine Clark. "The Classical Concept of *Head* as 'Source'." Pages 267–283 in Gretchen Gaebelein Hull. *Equal to Serve: Women and Men in the Church and Home.* Old Tappan, NJ: Revell, 1987.

Lampe, G. W. H., ed. *A Patristic Greek Lexicon.* Oxford: Clarendon, 1961. (PGL)

Lee, Dorothy A. *The Ministry of Women in the New Testament: Reclaiming the Biblical Vision for Church Leadership.* Grand Rapids: Baker, 2021.

Leo XIII, Pope. *Providentissimus Deu: Encyclical on the Study of Holy Scripture.* Nov. 18, 1893. https://www.vatican.va/content/leo-xiii/en/encyclicals/documents/hf_l-xiii_enc_18111893_providentissimus-deus.html

Liddell, Henry George and Robert Scott. *A Greek-English Lexicon.* Edited by Henry S. Jones and Roderick McKenzie. 9th ed. Oxford: Clarendon, 1940. With A Revised Supplement. Edited by P. G. W. Glare and A. A. Thompson, 1996. (LSJ)

Lowe, Stephen D. "Rethinking the Female Status/Function Question: The Jew/ Gentile Relationship as Paradigm." *Journal of the Evangelical Theological Society* 34, 1 (March, 1991) 59–75.

Metzger, Bruce M. "Recent Developments in the Textual Criticism of the New Testament." Pages 145–162 in *Historical and Literary Studies: Pagan, Jewish, and Christian.* NTTS 8; Leiden: Brill and Grand Rapids: Eerdmans, 1968.

Mickelsen, Alvera, ed. *Women, Authority & the Bible.* Downers Grove, IL: InterVarsity Press, 1986.

Montanari, F. *The Brill Dictionary of Ancient Greek.* English editors Madeleine Goh and Chad Schroeder. Leiden/Boston: Brill, 2015.

Moo, Douglas J. "1 Timothy 2:11–15: Meaning and Significance." *Trinity Journal* 1 (1980) 62–83.

_____. "The Interpretation of 1 Timothy 2:11–15: A Rejoinder." *Trinity Journal* 2 (1981) 198–222.

Moulton, James Hope. *An Introduction to the Study of New Testament Greek.* 5th ed. Revised by Henry G. Meecham. London: Epworth, 1955.

Moulton, James Hope and George Milligan. *The Vocabulary of the Greek Testament Illustrated from the Papyri and Other Non-Literary Sources.* London: Hodder and Stoughton, 1930 and Grand Rapids: Eerdmans, 1972.

Nestle, Eberhard and Erwin Nestle, *Novum Testamentum Graece.* Stuttgart: Württ. Bibelanstalt, 1953.

_____. *Novum Testamentum Graece Begründet von Eberrhard und Erwin Nestle.* Edited by Barbara and Kurt Aland, Johannes Karavidopoulos, Carlo M. Martini, Bruce M. Metzger. 28th edition. Stuttgart: Deutsche Bibelgesellschaft, 2012. (NA[28])

Oepke, A. "γυνή," TDNT 1:360–363. Ed. G. Kittel and G. Friedrich. Trans. G. W. Bromiley. 10 vols. Grand Rapids: Eerdmans, 1964–1976.

Ortlund, Raymond C., Jr. "Male-Female Equality and Male Headship: Genesis 1–3." Pages 95–112 in *Recovering Biblical Manhood and Womanhood: A Response to Evangelical Feminism.* Edited by John Piper and Wayne Grudem. Wheaton, IL: Crossway, 1991.

Pack, Roger A. *Artemidori Daldiani Onirocriticon Libri V.* Leipzig: Teubner, 1963.

Pape, Wilhelm. *Griechisch-Deutsches Handwörterbuch.* 3rd ed. 3 vols. Braunschweig: Fjriedrich Beiweg und Sohn, 1880.

Parker, David C. "Through a Screen Darkly: Digital Texts and the New Testament." *Journal of the Study of the New Testament* (2003) 395–411.

Passow, Franz. *Handwörterbuch der griechischen Sprache.* 1819–1824 revision of J. G. Schneider's lexicon. 1831 rev. ed. in Passow's name only. Rev. ed. Leipzig: Rost, Palm, and Kreussler, 1847.

Payne, Philip B. "1 Tim 2.12 and the Use of οὐδέ to Combine Two Elements to Express a Single Idea." *New Testament Studies* 54, 2 (2008) 235–253.

_____. "The Authenticity of the Parable of the Sower and its Interpretation." Pages 163–207 in *Gospel Perspectives: Studies of History and Tradition in the Four Gospels.* Edited by R. T. France and David Wenham. Sheffield: JSOT, 1980.

_____. "The Authenticity of the Parables of Jesus." Pages 329–344 in *Gospel Perspectives II.* Edited by R. T. France and David Wenham. Sheffield: JSOT, 1981.

_____. "A Critique of Thomas R. Schreiner's Review of Man and Woman, One in Christ." https://www.pbpayne.com/a-critique-of-thomas-r-schreiner's-review -of-man-and-woman-one-in-christ/

_____. "Critique of Vaticanus Distigme-obelos Denials." https://www.pbpayne .com/critique-of-vaticanus-distigme-obelos-denials/

_____. "Fuldensis, Sigla for Variants in Vaticanus, and 1 Cor 14.34–5." *New Testament Studies* 41 (1995) 240–262.

_____. "The Interpretation of 1 Timothy 2:11–15: A Surrejoinder." Pages 96–115 in Part II of *What Does the Scripture Teach About the Ordination of Women?* A study commissioned by the Committee on Ministerial Standing. Minneapolis: The Evangelical Free Church of America, 1986.

_____. "Is 1 Corinthians 14:34–35 a Marginal Comment or a Quotation? A Response to Kirk MacGregor." *Priscilla Papers* 33, 2 (Spring 2019) 24–30.

_____. "Libertarian Women in Ephesus: A Response to Douglas J. Moo's Article, '1 Timothy 2:11–15: Meaning and Significance.'" *Trinity Journal* 2 (1981) 169–197.

_____. *Man and Woman, One in Christ: An Exegetical and Theological Study of Paul's Letters*. Grand Rapids: Zondervan, 2009.

_____. "Ms. 88 as Evidence for a Text Without 1 Cor 14.34–5." *New Testament Studies* 44 (1998) 152–158.

_____. "The Order of Sowing and Ploughing in the Parable of the Sower." *New Testament Studies* 25 (1977–1978) 123–129.

_____. "Οὐδέ Combining Two Elements to Convey a Single Idea and 1 Timothy 2:12: Further Insights." Pages 24–34 in *Missing Voices*. Minneapolis: CBE International .org, 2015.

_____. "Response." Pages 118–132 in *Women, Authority & the Bible*. Ed. Alvera Mickelsen. Downers Grove, IL: InterVarsity, 1986.

_____. "The Seeming Inconsistency of the Interpretation of the Parable of the Sower." *New Testament Studies* 26 (1979–1980) 564–568.

_____. "The Text-Critical Function of the Umlauts in Vaticanus, with Special Attention to 1 Corinthians 14.34–35: A Response to J. Edward Miller." *Journal for the Study of the New Testament* 27, 1 (2004) 105–112.

_____. "Vaticanus Distigme-obelos Symbols Marking Added Text Including 1 Corinthians 14.34–5." *New Testament Studies* 63, 4 (October 2017) 604–625.

_____. "What About Headship? From Hierarchy to Equality." Pages 140–161, 226–232 in *Mutual by Design: A Better Model for Christian Marriage*. Elizabeth Beyer, ed. Minneapolis: CBE International, 2017.

_____. "What Does *Kephalē* Mean in the New Testament? Response." Pages 118–132 in *Women, Authority & the Bible*. Edited by Alvera Mickelsen. Downers Grove, IL: InterVarsity Press, 1986.

_____. "Wild Hair and Gender Equality in 1 Corinthians 11:20–16." *Priscilla Papers* 20, 3 (Summer 2006) 9–18. Witherington, Ben III. *Women and the Genesis of Christianity*. Cambridge: Cambridge University Press, 1990.

Payne, Philip B. and Paul Canart. "Distigmai Matching the Original Ink of Codex Vaticanus: Do they Mark the Location of Textual Variants?" Pages 199–226 in *Le manuscrit B de la Bible (Vaticanus graecus 1209) Introduction au fac-similé, Actes du Colloque de Genève (11 juin 2001), Contributions supplémentaires*. Edited by Patrick Andrist. Lausanne, Switzerland: Éditions du Zèbre, 2009.

Payne, Philip B. and Paul Canart. "The Originality of Text-Critical Symbols in Codex Vaticanus," *Novum Testamentum* 42, 2 (2000) 105–113.

Petrina, Henri. *Dictionarium Graecolatinum*. Basil: Henric Petrina, 1568.

Philo. Vol. 1 of 10 vols. Loeb Classical Library. Translated by Colson, F. H. and G. H. Whitaker. Cambridge, MA: Harvard University Press, 1929.

Philo. Vol. 4 of 10 vols. Loeb Classical Library. Translated by Colson, F. H. and G. H. Whitaker. Cambridge, MA: Harvard University Press, 1932.

Philo. Vol. 8 of 10 vols. Loeb Classical Library. Translated by F. H. Colson. Cambridge, MA: Harvard University Press, 1979.

Pidgeon, Kylie Maddox. "Complementarianism and Domestic Abuse: A Social-Science Perspective on Whether 'Equal but Different' is Really Equal at All." Pages 572–596 in *Discovering Biblical Equality: Biblical, Theological, Cultural, and Practical Perspectives.* 3rd ed. Edited by Ronald W. Pierce and Cynthia Long Westfall. Downers Grove, IL: InterVarsity, 2021.

Piper, John and Wayne Grudem, eds. *Recovering Biblical Manhood and Womanhood: A Response to Evangelical Feminism.* Wheaton, IL: Crossway, 1991.

Plutarch. *Plutarch's Moralia.* Translated by Frank Cole Babbitt. "Advice to Bride and Groom." Vol. 2 of 15 vols. Loeb Classical Library. Cambridge, MA: Harvard University Press, 1928.

Preisigke, Friedrich. *Wörterbuch der griechischen Papyrusurkunden,* Berlin: Selbstverlag des Verfassers, 1926–1931.

Renehan, R. *Greek Lexicographical Notes: A Critical Supplement to the Greek-English Lexicon of Liddell-Scott-Jones.* Hypomnemata 45. Göttingen: Vandenhoeck & Ruprecht, 1975.

Roberts, Alexander and James Donaldson, eds. *Nicene and Post Nicene Fathers, Series 1.* Grand Rapids: Eerdmans, 1989 reprint. (NFPF[1])

Robertson, A. T. *A Grammar of the Greek New Testament in the Light of Historical Research.* 4th edition. Nashville: Broadman, 1934.

Rost, Valentin Christian Friedrich. *Griechisch-Deutsches Wörterbuch.* Göttingen: Vandenhök & Ruprecht, 1818; Braunschweig: Westerman, 1959.

Ryrie, Charles Caldwell. *The Place of Women in the Church.* New York: Macmillan, 1958. Reprinted in paperback as *The Role of Women in the Church.* Chicago: Moody, 1958.

Sanders, E. P. "Testament of Abraham." Pages 869–902 in *Old Testament Pseudepigrapha.* Ed. J. H. Charlesworth. 2 vols. Garden City, NY: Doubleday, 1983.

Schenkl, Carlo. *Vocabolario Greco-Italiano.* Bologona: A. Mondadori, n.d.

Schironi, Francesca. "The Ambiguity of Signs: Critical ΣΗΜΕΙΑ from Zenodotus to Origen." Pages 87–112 in *Homer and the Bible in the Eyes of Ancient Interpreters.* Edited by M. R. Niehoff. Leiden/Boston: Brill, 2012.

Schmid, Ulrich. "Conceptualizing "Scribal" Performances: Reader's Notes." Pages 49–64 in *The Textual History of the Greek New Testament: Changing Views in Contemporary Research.* Edited by K. Wachtel and M. Holmes. Atlanta: SBL, 2011.

Schneider, J. G. *Handwörterbuch der griechischen Sprache.* 4th ed. 2 vols. Leipzig: Friedrich Christian Wilhelm Vogel, 1831. 5th ed. 1847.

Schreiner, Thomas R. "Philip Payne on Familiar Ground: A Review of Philip B. Payne, *Man and Woman, One in Christ*." *Journal for Biblical Manhood and Womanhood* 15, 1 (2010) 33–46. Payne's response is at https://www.pbpayne.com/a-critique-of-thomas-r-schreiner's-review-of-man-and-woman-one-in-christ/.

_____. "The Valuable Ministries of Women in the Context of Male Leadership: A Survey of Old and New Testament Examples and Teaching." Pages 209–232 in *Recovering Biblical Manhood and Womanhood: A Response to Evangelical Feminism*. Edited by John Piper and Wayne Grudem. Wheaton, IL: Crossway, 1991.

The Septuagint Version of the Old Testament with an English Translation. Grand Rapids: Zondervan, 1970.

Souter, Alexander. *Novum Testamentum Graece*. Oxford: Clarendon, 1910.

Spencer, Aída Besançon, *2 Timothy and Titus*. New Covenant Commentary Series. Eugene, OR: Wipf & Stock, 2014.

_____. "Leadership of Women in Crete and Macedonia as a Model for the Church." *Priscilla Papers* 27, 4 (Autumn 2013) 5–15.

Staab, Karl, ed. *Pauluskommentare aus der griechischen Kirche aus Katenenhandschriften gesammelt und herausgegeben: Fragmenta commentarii in Rom.–2 Cor. Neutestamentliche Abhandlungen* 15. Münster: Aschendorff, 1933.

Stuttard, David. *Nemesis: Alcibiades and the Fall of Athens*. Cambridge, MA: Harvard University Press, 2018.

Swanson, Reuben J. *New Testament Greek Manuscripts: Variant Readings Arranged in Horizontal Lines Against Codex Vaticanus: 1 Corinthians*. Wheaton, IL: Tyndale House and Padasena, CA: William Carey International University Press, 2003.

_____. *New Testament Greek Manuscripts: Variant Readings Arranged in Horizontal Lines Against Codex Vaticanus: Acts*. Sheffield: Sheffield Academic Press and Padasena, CA: William Carey International University Press, 1998.

_____. *New Testament Greek Manuscripts: Variant Readings Arranged in Horizontal Lines Against Codex Vaticanus: John*. Sheffield: Sheffield Academic Press and Padasena, CA: William Carey International University Press, 1995.

_____. *New Testament Greek Manuscripts: Variant Readings Arranged in Horizontal Lines Against Codex Vaticanus: Luke*. Sheffield: Sheffield Academic Press and Padasena, CA: William Carey International University Press, 1995.

_____. *New Testament Greek Manuscripts: Variant Readings Arranged in Horizontal Lines Against Codex Vaticanus: Mark*. Sheffield: Sheffield Academic Press and Padasena, CA: William Carey International University Press, 1995.

_____. *New Testament Greek Manuscripts: Variant Readings Arranged in Horizontal Lines Against Codex Vaticanus: Matthew*. Sheffield: Sheffield Academic Press and Padasena, CA: William Carey International University Press, 1995.

Tasker, R. V. G. *The Greek New Testament, Being the Text Translated in The New English Bible 1961*. Cambridge: Cambridge University Press, 1964.

Thiselton, Anthony C. *The First Epistle to the Corinthians.* New International Greek Testament Commentary. Grand Rapids: Eerdmans, 2000.

Thompson, Cynthia L. "Hairstyles, Head-coverings, and St. Paul. Portraits from Roman Corinth." *Biblical Archaeologist* 51, 2 (June, 1988) 99–115.

Tischendorf, Constantine. *Novum Testamentum Graece.* 8th ed. 3 vols. Leipzig: Giesecke & Devrient, 1869–1894.

Westcott, Brooke Foss and F. J. A. Hort. *The New Testament in the Original Greek.* 2 vols. London: Macmillan, 1881–1982. 2nd edition, 1896.

White, Robert J. *The Interpretation of Dreams.* Park Ridge, NJ: Noyes, 1975.

Witherington, Ben, III. *Women and the Genesis of Christianity.* Cambridge: Cambridge University Press, 1990.

Woodhouse, S. C. *English-Greek Dictionary: A Vocabulary of the Attic Language.* London: George Routledge & Sons, 1932.

Zonaras, Johannes. *Lexicon.* Edited by Johann August Henrich Tittmann. Leipzig: S. Siegfr. Lebr. Crusii, 1808.